# Récital 1961

# 33 1/3 Global

**33 1/3 Global**, a series related to but independent from **33 1/3**, takes the format of the original series of short, music-based books and brings the focus to music throughout the world. With initial volumes focusing on Japanese and Brazilian music, the series will also include volumes on the popular music of Australia/Oceania, Europe, Africa, the Middle East, and more.

## 33 1/3 Japan

Series Editor: Noriko Manabe

Spanning a range of artists and genres – from the 1970s rock of Happy End to technopop band Yellow Magic Orchestra, the Shibuya-kei of Cornelius, classic anime series *Cowboy Bebop,* J-Pop/EDM hybrid Perfume, and vocaloid star Hatsune Miku – 33 1/3 Japan is a series devoted to in-depth examination of Japanese popular music of the twentieth and twenty-first centuries.

Published Titles:

Supercell's *Supercell* by Keisuke Yamada

Yoko Kanno's *Cowboy Bebop Soundtrack* by Rose Bridges

Perfume's *Game* by Patrick St. Michel

Cornelius's *Fantasma* by Martin Roberts

Joe Hisaishi's *My Neighbor Totoro: Soundtrack* by Kunio Hara

Shonen Knife's *Happy Hour* by Brooke McCorkle

Nenes' *Koza Dabasa* by Henry Johnson

Yuming's *The 14th Moon* by Lasse Lehtonen

Forthcoming Titles:

Yellow Magic Orchestra's *Yellow Magic Orchestra* by Toshiyuki Ohwada

Kohaku utagassen: The Red and White Song Contest by Shelley Brunt

## 33 1/3 Brazil

Series Editor: Jason Stanyek

Covering the genres of samba, tropicália, rock, hip hop, forró, bossa nova, heavy metal and funk, among others, 33 1/3 Brazil is a series devoted to in-depth examination of the most important Brazilian albums of the twentieth and twenty-first centuries.

Published Titles:
Caetano Veloso's *A Foreign Sound* by Barbara Browning
Tim Maia's *Tim Maia Racional Vols. 1 &2* by Allen Thayer
João Gilberto and Stan Getz's *Getz/Gilberto* by Brian McCann
Gilberto Gil's *Refazenda* by Marc A. Hertzman
Dona Ivone Lara's *Sorriso Negro* by Mila Burns
Milton Nascimento and Lô Borges's *The Corner Club* by Jonathon
    Grasse
Racionais MCs' *Sobrevivendo no Inferno* by Derek Pardue
Naná Vasconcelos's *Saudades* by Daniel B. Sharp
Chico Buarque's First *Chico Buarque* by Charles A. Perrone

Forthcoming titles:
Jorge Ben Jor's *África Brasil* by Frederick J. Moehn

## 33 1/3 Europe

Series Editor: Fabian Holt
Spanning a range of artists and genres, 33 1/3 Europe offers engaging accounts of popular and culturally significant albums of Continental Europe and the North Atlantic from the twentieth and twenty-first centuries.

Published Titles:
Darkthrone's *A Blaze in the Northern Sky* by Ross Hagen
Ivo Papazov's *Balkanology* by Carol Silverman
Heiner Müller and Heiner Goebbels's *Wolokolamsker Chaussee* by
    Philip V. Bohlman
Modeselektor's *Happy Birthday!* by Sean Nye
Mercyful Fate's *Don't Break the Oath* by Henrik Marstal
Bea Playa's *I'll Be Your Plaything* by Anna Szemere and András Rónai
Various Artists' *DJs do Guetto* by Richard Elliott
Czesław Niemen's *Niemen Enigmatic* by Ewa Mazierska and Mariusz
    Gradowski

Massada's *Astaganaga* by Lutgard Mutsaers
Los Rodriguez's *Sin Documentos* by Fernán del Val and Héctor Fouce
Édith Piaf's *Récital 1961* by David Looseley

Forthcoming Titles:
Nuovo Canzoniere Italiano's *Bella Ciao* by Jacopo Tomatis
Amália Rodrigues's *Amália at the Olympia* by Lilla Ellen Gray
Ardit Gjebrea's *Projekt Jon* by Nicholas Tochka
Vopli Vidopliassova's *Tantsi* by Maria Sonevytsky
Iannis Xenakis' *Persepolis* by Aram Yardumian

## 33 1/3 Oceania

Series Editors: Jon Stratton (senior editor) and Jon Dale (specializing in books on albums from Aotearoa/New Zealand)

Spanning a range of artists and genres from Australian Indigenous artists to Maori and Pasifika artists, from Aotearoa/New Zealand noise music to Australian rock, and including music from Papua and other Pacific islands, 33 1/3 Oceania offers exciting accounts of albums that illustrate the wide range of music made in the Oceania region.

Published Titles:
John Farnham's *Whispering Jack* by Graeme Turner
The Church's *Starfish* by Chris Gibson
Regurgitator's *Unit* by Lachlan Goold and Lauren Istvandity

Forthcoming Titles:
Ed Kuepper's *Honey Steel's Gold* by John Encarnacao
Kylie Minogue's *Kylie* by Adrian Renzo and Liz Giuffre
Space Waltz's *Space Waltz* by Ian Chapman
The Dead C's *Clyma est mort* by Darren Jorgensen
Chain's *Toward the Blues* by Peter Beilharz
Bic Runga's *The Drive* by Henry Johnson
The Front Lawn's *Songs from the Front Lawn* by Matthew Bannister

# Récital 1961

David Looseley

Series Editor: Fabian Holt

BLOOMSBURY ACADEMIC
NEW YORK • LONDON • OXFORD • NEW DELHI • SYDNEY

BLOOMSBURY ACADEMIC
Bloomsbury Publishing Inc
1385 Broadway, New York, NY 10018, USA
50 Bedford Square, London, WC1B 3DP, UK
29 Earlsfort Terrace, Dublin 2, Ireland

BLOOMSBURY, BLOOMSBURY ACADEMIC and the Diana logo
aretrademarks of Bloomsbury Publishing Plc

First published in the United States of America 2023

For legal purposes the Acknowledgements on p. x constitute an
extension of this copyright page.

Cover design: Louise Dugdale
Cover image © 333sound.com

Bloomsbury Publishing Inc does not have any control over, or responsibility for,
any third-party websites referred to or in this book. All internet addresses given
in this book were correct at the time of going to press. The author and publisher
regret any inconvenience caused if addresses have changed or sites have
ceased to exist, but can accept no responsibility for any such changes.

Whilst every effort has been made to locate copyright holders the publishers
would be grateful to hear from any person(s) not here acknowledged.

Library of Congress Cataloging-in-Publication Data

Names: Looseley, David, author.
Title: Récital 1961 / David Looseley.
Description: [1st.] | New York : Bloomsbury Academic, 2023. |
Series: 33 1/3 Europe | Includes bibliographical references and index. |
Summary: "Examines Édith Piaf's live album Recital 1961, recorded at the
famous Paris Olympia, and explores why it marked the last great turning
point in her career"– Provided by publisher.
Identifiers: LCCN 2022022599 (print) | LCCN 2022022600 (ebook) |
ISBN 9781501362118 (hardback) | ISBN 9781501362101 (paperback) |
ISBN 9781501362125 (epub) | ISBN 9781501362132 (pdf) | ISBN 9781501362149
Subjects: LCSH: Piaf, Edith, 1915–1963. Récital 1961. |
Popular music–France–1961–1970–History and criticism.
Classification: LCC ML420.P52 L666 2023  (print) |
LCC ML420.P52 (ebook) | DDC 781.640944–dc23/eng/20220511
LC record available at https://lccn.loc.gov/2022022599
LC ebook record available at https://lccn.loc.gov/2022022600

ISBN:     HB:      978-1-5013-6211-8
          PB:      978-1-5013-6210-1
          ePDF:    978-1-5013-6213-2
          eBook:   978-1-5013-6212-5

Typeset by Integra Software Services Pvt. Ltd.
Printed and bound in Great Britain

Series: 33 1/3 Europe

To find out more about our authors and books visit www.bloomsbury.com
and sign up for our newsletters.

*For my grandson*
*Ben Looseley-Burnet*
*with love*

# Contents

# Acknowledgements

I'm very grateful to the following, who have variously provided advice, information, thoughts, recollections and other forms of help with this book: Dr Nigel Armstrong, Ewan Burnet, Sylvain Cornil-Frerrot, Charles Dumont, Fabrice Ferment, Dr Fabian Holt, Dr Rachel Haworth, Dr Barbara Lebrun, Florence Lemaître, Dr Isabelle Marc, Professor Sue Miller, Doudou Morizot.

As always, I also wish to acknowledge my special debt to the late David Whale, whom I never met, and to his widow Ann who in donating to me David's vast collection of books, CDs and documents on French chanson has helped my work immeasurably.

Lastly, I express my gratitude to Avril Looseley for reading and discussing the book with such insight and enthusiasm, bringing to bear on it her deep knowledge of France and French and her love of chanson.

# 1 Imagining Piaf

One late evening in 1960, a spectral figure stands watchfully behind the closed curtain of the Paris Olympia. Tiny, stooped and ashen, she steps forward, moving in slow motion as if she might break at any moment. It's Thursday 29 December and Édith Piaf has just turned forty-five. Three months before, the prospect of her performing to that vast, formidable auditorium would have been unthinkable. Yet the engagement that began that night was to last a remarkable three months and would be her greatest triumph. The concert was audio-recorded and an edited version rushed out on vinyl the following month, with the laconic title *Récital 1961*.[1] This book tells the story of that historic first show and the album that, by preserving it, has inflected how she's been remembered ever since.

The recital was a turning point in several ways. Promoted as 'the event of the year', it was her first live performance in just over twelve months after potentially fatal illness, and her audience that night had an extraordinary if ambiguous response to this unforeseen comeback. The record's sales were also exceptional. It became the biggest seller of the new releases in France at the start of 1961,[2] the first pressing apparently selling out in just five days.[3] By the end of the decade, it had sold 175,000 copies. This doesn't sound much today but in France, where the market for LPs was particularly small (sales very rarely exceeded 200,000),[4] the album confirmed her as a hot property of the record industry. But three exhilarating weeks into the run, her health started to fail again and she was hospitalized soon after it ended. She would be booked there one last time in autumn 1962 but a year later she was dead. The December 1960 comeback, then, was no ordinary triumph: she'd had plenty of those. She'd already appeared at the Olympia itself in 1955, 1956 and 1958. All three engagements had been sell-outs and generated live albums.[5] But this particular show was of a different order. And the album which preserves it stands as a biographical full stop and a posthumous new paragraph in one of the great narratives of global popular culture. It's also a snapshot of a music scene and a whole culture on the threshold of change.

I've already written about the processes that have turned Piaf into the transnational myth she is today.[6] Now as then, my own cultural perspective shapes the way I think about those processes. I'm interested in what, if anything, might be seen as singularly 'French' or 'European' about this myth. Perhaps this is because I'm a native inhabitant of the UK where in 2016 a slim majority decided they no longer wanted to identify with Europe, whereas I persist in thinking of myself post-Brexit as British-European. Which means I view Europe and specifically France from a liminal space: I'm both outsider and insider yet neither entirely. And I can only view Piaf through the same intercultural lens. Having trained as a linguist, I'm especially intrigued by the rhetorical formations, francophone and anglophone, that have turned her into what she is today. The Olympia concert sheds light on these formations generally but also has a significance of its own, not least because of the album. *Récital 1961* doesn't only preserve a performance: it constructs Piaf on the threshold of posterity. I want to probe that significance, suggesting why the concert seemed to mean so much to audiences at the time and what the LP has contributed to the way it's remembered.

Over six decades later, this isn't easy. Some of my suggestions will have to be more speculative than others given the shortage of the kinds of empirical evidence historians usually rely on. But the more capacious brief of the 33 1/3 series makes it a good place to try those ideas out. I also want to address the cultural and historical contexts of the concert and the album because I don't think we can fully understand her comeback without them. And again the ambition of the 33 1/3 Europe sub-series, which is to look at popular musics in European cultural history exactly matches my own.

The concert was instantly conspicuous because of the conjunction of artist and venue. But a third component has intervened postmortem in that her subsequent relapse and death give it a different narrative shape. Like a Greek tragedy, her zenith heralded her nadir. To understand how, we need to look at the Piaf story up to 1960 and the place of the Olympia in it. But we also have to be aware that the story is a kind of autofiction. The 'real' Piaf, according to friends, colleagues and lovers, was many things at once: gifted, fun-loving, cruel, despotic, intelligent, superstitious, generous, needy. But although much in their accounts is factual, the facts were constantly being edited into a narrative and performed by Piaf herself, both on stage and off. Then there's the exponential re-editing of that edited narrative, by those same friends, colleagues and lovers, as well as the media, biographers, tributes, plays and films. More than most celebrities, the artist formerly known as Édith Piaf has become a cultural artefact. The Piaf we think we know is imagined. She was a work in progress from the outset and, as we'll see, *Récital 1961* is the culmination of that work in her lifetime. With her death and the passing of six decades, she's become a free-floating signifier, open to ever more creative recounting and infinite reinterpretation, albeit through the prism of a few core narrative threads.[7] For these reasons, the rest of this chapter can only unspool those threads that take us to the watershed moment of 29 December 1960.

Piaf was born Édith Gassion in Belleville, a working-class district of Paris, on 19 December 1915: not, apparently, in the street as legend would have it but in a local hospital. Her mother, known professionally as Line Marsa, was a street singer of French, Italian and Moroccan-Berber heritage, her father a travelling circus contortionist. Édith grew up with little parental stability and, after living in her grandmother's brothel for a time, spent much of her childhood on the road, singing to passers-by as part of her father's act. In her teens, she went solo, with a friend who passed the hat. At seventeen, she had a child out of wedlock, who died two years later. Her professional career began that same year, in 1935, just as the French music industry was taking shape thanks to recording, radio and cinema. She was given the stage name Piaf, Parisian slang for 'sparrow', by her first impresario, Louis Leplée, who heard her singing on a street corner. He ran an upmarket club called Le Gerny's, where he announced his new discovery as 'La Môme Piaf' (Kid Piaf or, more commonly, the Little Sparrow). But in 1936 he was mysteriously murdered, leaving Édith unmentored and exposed to the lowlife milieu she already frequented, until she was taken up by a new manager, Raymond Asso, who also became her lover. He coached her, meticulously and at times violently, though her years working the streets had already taught her how to tug at the heartstrings of passers-by using the visual pathos of social exclusion: her tender years, her gender, her distressed appearance and diminutive stature (she was well under five feet tall). From the start, her act was knowingly built on the contrast between an exposed body and a self-possessed voice. And, from around 1937, nobody knew better how to engineer and exploit this contrast than Piaf herself.

There's a tendency in the English-speaking world to think of her as a cabaret singer, with the echoes that word has of intimate, bohemian nightclubs in left-bank Paris or pre-war Berlin.[8] This isn't exactly the case. She did get her breakthrough in Leplée's cabaret and would perform in similar venues from time to time. But from 1937, her reputation was made in music halls, mostly situated on the more affluent right bank. She did, though, maintain a cabaret-style intimacy with her audiences, even on those vast stages. Asso encouraged this and wrote material for her to match. His spare, dramatic narratives were set to music by Marguerite Monnot, a classically trained composer who would work with Édith for the next twenty-five years. Asso himself had a shorter shelf life, though he was responsible for a further name change. In November 1937, at her second booking at the prestigious ABC, a 1200-seater music hall, she was announced with a new stage identity: 'La Môme is dead. What you're about to hear is Édith Piaf!'[9]

This initial team – Piaf, Asso and Monnot – sculpted the persona that would lodge in public perceptions and, with modifications, last throughout her career and into her afterlives. As the years went by, new management and support staff, musicians, arrangers, photographers, biographers, media people, and above all lyricists and composers – all tightly controlled by the singer herself – would fine-tune the imagined Piaf, turning her into the prototype of the modern diva. So too did her serial affairs, which she seemed only too happy to publicize. Her official photographer in the late 1950s, Hugues Vassal, met her when she rang his newspaper, the gossipy *France Dimanche*, which always turned to her for celebrity stories. She was performing in Dijon and changing lovers, she announced, so they were to send a photographer to snap the new man along with the old. And she demanded the front page.[10] A number of male stars launched their careers by providing her with sexual or other services and she made a habit of pressuring young men she liked the look of to become singers. At various times, Charles Aznavour, Yves Montand, the American singer and actor Eddie Constantine, Georges Moustaki, Charles Dumont and a host of writers and composers were indebted to her.[11] They have been called the 'Piaf nebula' and their musical cross-fertilizations have ramified up to the present day.[12] Women, however, were largely excluded. With the odd exception like Marlene Dietrich and Monnot, Piaf was wary of her own gender and, with rivals, downright hostile.

Through minute image management, careful choice of songs and permanent self-awareness onstage and off, she authored a virtual life story, a USP whose constants were heartbreak, tragedy and an uncrushable faith in love, not so much giving the public what they wanted as making them want what she gave. The Olympia show of December 1960 was the climax of this self-invention. But the one element she couldn't manipulate was destiny.

After she'd conquered America in 1947–8, her career went global and for the next fifteen years or so touring became her life. Two key twists in the narrative emerge from this frantic activity. The first was her affair with the boxer Marcel Cerdan, which began in New York in late 1947. Their doomed idyll is well known, chiefly because of Piaf's retelling of it. While dating her, Cerdan became world middleweight champion in 1948 but lost his title the following year to Jake LaMotta, the Raging Bull. While training to win it back, he went home to his wife and children in Casablanca. The return match was set for

2 December 1949, so from there he set off for Paris ready to set sail for the States. But Édith, furious that he'd left her for his wife, begged him to return by plane, despite his aversion to air travel. On 27 October, he took off from Orly but never arrived. The plane crashed into a mountain in the Azores, killing all forty-eight people on board. Devastated, Piaf still performed that evening at the Versailles Club in midtown Manhattan but reportedly collapsed halfway through the self-penned song 'Hymne à l'amour' (Hymn to Love, adapted as 'If You Love Me'), written before Cerdan's death but forever associated with it.

If he'd lived, who knows whether he'd have gone the way of all her temporary lovers? But in death, he became the unique male lead in her self-penned drama. Certainly, from this point on – and this is the second twist in the narrative – her health declined. As well as the bereavement, the onset of chronic rheumatism and five car accidents in the 1950s contributed to her growing addiction to morphine and alcohol. Throughout the decade, her demonic schedule of touring, recording, media appearances and filming (she appeared in five movies between 1951 and 1958) left her exhausted. The period from 1958 to October 1960 was particularly dark, with repeat hospitalizations and failed affairs. In February 1959, she was taken ill twice at Manhattan's Waldorf Astoria and underwent an operation. Returning to France in June to start a summer tour, she was back in hospital by September. After only a brief convalescence, she was on the road again with what the press dubbed her suicide tour. Collapsing on stage in December 1959, she was then in and out of hospital for the next six months and unfit to perform, cancelling a planned tour and an Olympia booking for October 1960. Although she'd been well enough to work on a new studio album in May, neither she nor her entourage believed she would ever perform live again and she became seriously depressed. It's at this epic low point that she heard the song that would change her life.

'Non, je ne regrette rien' ('No Regrets') was written by a regular member of the Piaf nebula, the lyricist Michel Vaucaire, and the composer Charles Dumont, a successful tunesmith for established stars like Tino Rossi and newcomers like Dalida but an outsider to Piaf's circle. For some reason, she didn't like him and had turned down his melodies so unceremoniously that he'd promised never to have anything to do with her. When Vaucaire revealed he'd penned the lyric with her in mind, Dumont took some persuading but he eventually agreed and an appointment was made. Fate then took a hand. At the last minute, she tried to cancel the meeting but the pair didn't get the message and innocently showed up at her flat. She kept them waiting an hour, finally emerging clad in a scruffy dressing gown, looking frail and irritated and barking at them to make it quick. Even more convinced he should never have come, Dumont angrily thumped out the tune on her piano and merely spoke the words. Judging by her face, he expected her to slam the lid down on his fingers at any moment. But something astonishing happened. Visibly surprised that the melody was by him, she asked to hear it again. 'As if by magic all the lines of illness seemed to fall from her face, and her attitude towards me changed alarmingly. *Then* it was as if we'd been friends her whole life.'[13] He was made to play it over and over until he and Vaucaire were finally allowed home, only to be recalled after midnight to repeat the performance until dawn. The song, she declared grandly, was her story. She predicted it would go around the world and follow Dumont for the rest of his life.[14] She was right.

There's obviously some further myth-building at work in this well-rehearsed tale. She'd already declared the month before that she was recovering and promised she'd be back at the Olympia by December.[15] Throughout September and October, between therapeutic sessions with her chiropractor Lucien Vaimber, she'd been rehearsing, toing and froing between Paris and the country, recording a radio show, and going to the theatre and cinema. On 11 November, she did indeed sign to appear at the Olympia for six weeks from December. The venue's manager, Bruno Coquatrix, who'd been present when Dumont had played her the song, was elated. Virtually ruined, he'd been pleading with her manager Loulou Barrier to let her appear, saying she alone could rescue him from the bailiffs.[16] She had financial problems of her own after years of reckless spending, but above all she saw the comeback as a turning point in her destiny. She prepared for it with unparalleled dedication, learning the new songs, working out how to stage them, micro-managing lighting, sound, curtain falls and the position of each musician. She bullied everyone into a merciless rehearsal schedule in her flat, that started late afternoon once she'd got up and went on long into the night. 'Boulevard Lannes was just like a mad-house', a companion recalled. 'Well-wishers filed in and out all day, most of them unsure whether they were helping Piaf prepare for a comeback or encouraging her towards an early grave.'[17] She commissioned new songs from another of her stable, Michel Rivgauche, and of course Vaucaire and Dumont, jettisoning all but one of the Monnot tunes she'd originally lined up for her Olympia return. Marguerite was heartbroken. She died the following October at only fifty-eight. Like Aznavour before him, Dumont now became Édith's court favourite and platonic attendant. And, as ever, she made him a singer by duetting with him on the song they wrote together, 'Les Amants' (The lovers), launching a successful performing career that continued well into the twenty-first century.

Ahead of the Olympia, she did four warm-up shows. The first took place in Rheims on 17 December in front of a throng of media people hoping to scoop an onstage collapse or worse. Then came Nancy on the 18th, Thionville on the 19th (her 45th birthday), and Chaumont on the 20th, where a first recording was made but not released. On the 28th, she did a preview at the Cyrano cinema in Versailles. But it was only on the historic 29th that the show could be deemed 'created' – the French term for a first public performance. For a comeback of this magnitude, she had to be crowned at a major venue in the capital. She did some advance publicity for the show in an interview on 2 December on the popular *Cinq colonnes à la une* (Five columns on the front page), fronted by Pierre Desgraupes, where she performed 'Non, je ne regrette rien'.[18] The performance itself was powerful but during the interview she looked startlingly frail and detached, as if haunted by demons. The camera's unforgiving close-ups and Desgraupes's leading questions felt intrusive, fuelling media and public speculation about the concert itself, an unpleasant blend of adulation and prurience. Would she summon the old magic? Would she humiliate herself in front of two thousand spectators? Would she die on stage?

As it turned out, her return to the Olympia was her finest hour and a major cultural landmark. It was a benefit concert for the former First Free French Division (1ère DFL), the main infantry unit of the Resistance forces set up under de Gaulle in 1940, with some profits from programme sales going to the veterans' association. The first-night audience was appropriately distinguished. Pierre Messmer – Armed Forces minister, ex-legionnaire and future prime minister – was there, along with other ministers, army generals, prefects, ambassadors and celebrities: Zizi Jeanmaire, Georges Brassens, Lucienne

Boyer, Melina Mercouri.[19] There was a master of ceremonies, the comic actor Jean-Marie Proslier, and the show followed the music-hall tradition of a first half taken by other acts: a juggler (Ugo Garrido), the illusionist Aldo Richiardi who 'cut the woman in half', acrobatic dancers called the Lucky Latinos, the impersonator Claude Véga, and two singers: her lyricist Michel Rivgauche and her friend, songwriter and reputedly lover Julien Bouquet. She herself only took to the stage after the intermission, accompanied by around ten musicians, including her faithful accordionist Marc Bonel, another one-time lover Jacques Liébrard on guitar, the jazz harmonica player Dany Kane, a pianist and a small backing group, all conducted by the pianist Jacques Lesage, who replaced her usual arranger Robert Chauvigny but used his arrangements.

Before curtain-up, she devised a superstitious ritual that would continue every night. The Olympia's stage manager Doudou Morizot, her friend and lucky charm, had to escort her on his arm from her dressing room. She walked unsteadily, smiling at people in the wings, but then centring down as she reached the closed curtain. Her orchestra and all the technical staff stood in her honour. She kissed the little gold crucifix she always wore round her neck and crossed her fingers. Then she stood to attention, hands stiffly by her sides, eyes closed. This was the signal for Morizot to open the curtain.[20] There was a loud drum roll and a short introduction by Proslier, then the band, on stage behind her but half-hidden behind a tulle curtain, struck up 'Hymne à l'amour', her signature tune.

As the curtain opened, she walked slowly towards the microphone, clad in the iconic plain black dress which for one observer made her look like a waitress in an old-fashioned tea room.[21] A new one had in fact been designed specially for the occasion by Lanvin's celebrated designer Antonio Castillo, but she'd dismissed it in favour of the one she'd worn many times, smelling of mothballs.[22] Brand new shoes had similarly been swapped for an old pair that didn't hurt her feet. The crowd rose as one, applauding wildly with cries of encouragement for a good fifteen minutes.[23] 'Édith!', they called out. 'You're back', 'bravo', 'we love you'. She smiled graciously, with composure, then started working through her setlist of ten new songs, each announced soberly and clearly with the name of the lyricist and composer, followed by the title.

The power she exerted that night became cumulative: the audience grew more excited, more vocal, more in thrall. Watching from the wings, the journalist Jean Noli would later write: 'With each song, waves of applause swept towards her, ever more powerful and prolonged, issuing from an audience carried away by genuine emotional hysteria.'[24] The performance lasted just under an hour. There were countless calls for encores, so she reprised some old favourites, including 'La Foule' (The crowd), 'Milord' and 'Hymne à l'amour'. Memories are hazy but Morizot thinks she also sang 'Non, je ne regrette rien' a second time at some point, while Dumont believes she did so as her very last encore.[25] Before finally letting her go, spectators gave her a standing ovation, called to her, chanted, threw flowers. Father Christmas, impersonated by the famous actor Jean Marais, brought her a huge bouquet of roses. There were up to thirty curtain calls (accounts vary a good deal) and the show continued past midnight, finishing with what one commentator claims to be the longest standing ovation in the history of music hall.[26]

Four days later, on 2 January 1961, came the gala premiere which offered celebrities the chance to be seen: among them, Arletty, Marlene Dietrich, Roger Vadim, Claude Chabrol, Alain Delon and Romy Schneider, Dalida, Jean-Paul Belmondo, Paul

Newman, Louis Armstrong, Duke Ellington. Reactions were just as ecstatic. From then on, fans ready to pay between 3000 and 4000 old francs for a ticket would fill the hall night after night and seats had to be booked weeks in advance. Coquatrix implored her to extend the six-week engagement, which she contracted to do on 1 February 1961, even though by then her health was deteriorating and she needed a nightly injection of stimulant. By 24 March, almost three months after her début, exhaustion had set in, as well as irritation at Coquatrix's failure to agree a closing date. She pointedly took five days off at Vaimber's insistence, though even then, Coquatrix, ever the businessman, persuaded her to make up the lost time by doing just one more week, from 29 March to 6 April. Just before the final show, he sent her a note admitting to feeling guilty for what he'd urged her to do without regard for her well-being. 'I know it was mainly for me that you did that and, instead of feeling proud that you did, I feel a bit ashamed.'[27]

The shame wasn't misplaced. By the end, both he and Dumont needed to help her on and off stage behind the curtain. Her new lease of life the previous autumn had in fact come at a cost. Even so, taking only a week's rest, she took up touring again, starting in Lyon and then Brussels. Throughout May, she was criss-crossing the country almost nightly. Dumont sometimes had to carry her from car to dressing room. Her voice had also worsened, as had her reliance on drugs despite the apparently miraculous ministrations of Vaimber. To avoid the restrictions he imposed on her, she would resort to other, more compliant medical advisers and became addicted again. On 24 May, she was hospitalized for another major operation, her eighth in the previous thirty months, and yet again in June and July. When she was discharged, she was emaciated. That summer of 1961, her manager was forced to cancel some prestigious bookings, including Moscow. But even in convalescence, she carried on working at her legend, with the help of journalist Jean Noli who would publish her recollections in *France Dimanche*, then in a ghosted autobiography, *My Life*.[28]

On 15 June 1962, thirteen months after her last live performance, she began another comeback tour, culminating in a new booking at the Olympia that autumn which, to some disapproval, featured her young fiancé Théo Sarapo, whom she would marry in the course of the run on 9 October, duetting with him on stage that same evening on her final big hit 'A quoi ça sert l'amour' (What use is love?). This stint of almost a month (27 September to 23 October) would be her last at the venue she had become so intimately identified with. The crowds applauded wildly again and the shows sold out. On her very last night there, the stars came out dutifully to mark the event: Montand with his wife Simone Signoret, Sacha Distel, Serge Gainsbourg, and the young rocker Johnny Hallyday, who was moved to tears. She was not on form: exhausted, her face puffy from medication and her voice less assured. Morizot observed her slumped forward on a stool watching Sarapo from the wings, almost unable to keep upright: 'It was heartbreaking to see her looking so pitiful.'[29] Alongside vicious reporting of her marriage to Sarapo, who was still in his twenties, some reviewers were less forgiving than usual, complaining she was out of tune or that her material was dated. There was an embryonic sense that her time was up.

Her last ever live performance took place in Lille at the end of March 1963, poignantly to only a small house because of a transport strike. Ten days later she was again rushed to hospital for a blood transfusion and went into a coma. She revived enough to head south to convalesce, where she died on 10 October, a year and a day after her marriage. Still servicing her myth to the very end, her entourage had her body secretly transported back to Paris so that it could be said that she'd died in the city she had always symbolized. 100,000 people queued outside her apartment to view her embalmed body. The church denied her a religious funeral but 40,000 people turned out to see her buried in the historic Père Lachaise cemetery, resting place of many of France's most revered daughters and sons. Today, there's a Piaf museum, a Piaf statue and a Piaf audio tour of the city. A rose has been named after her. Her grave, in which Sarapo also lies, is a place of pilgrimage, always adorned with flowers. It's said that if you listen hard enough, you'll hear Édith and Théo whispering words of love.

The 1960 comeback, then, was her last truly memorable triumph and in effect her swan song. It was also the start of her posthumous myth, just as it became part of the mythology of the Olympia itself and of French popular music generally. In the next chapter, I'll look more closely at why.

# **2**   The Recital

'What happened that evening was close to being inexpressible', Dumont recalls. 'Long after, when I think about it, I still tell myself that consecration like that was nigh-on impossible.' Piaf herself told him his songs had made 29 December 1960 'the greatest night of my career'.[1] So, before looking at the album, we need to dig deeper into what made the show so extraordinary. I'll approach that question by asking three others. What personal meanings did Piaf have or acquire? What was the significance of the Olympia and its place within French popular music? And the most neglected and complex question of all: what was the impact of the momentous political circumstances prevailing in France at that moment – circumstances as volatile as Piaf's own? Might there be a case for suggesting that this shared volatility is reflected at some subliminal level in the extraordinary power of the show? That the perceived destinies of singer, venue and nation somehow became entwined?

## **Personal meanings**

Piaf's return consolidated her iconic status but also reshaped it. This was partly down to repertoire. Eye-witness accounts vary but it looks as though she prepared a set of fourteen or fifteen songs altogether, not all performed at any one time. Although she reprised some of her best loved numbers, it was the new ones that bore all the signifying weight. As the booking was extended, she would adjust these a little. 'Boulevard du crime' (Rivgauche-Léveillée), 'La Vie, l'amour' (Rivgauche-Chauvigny) and 'T'es l'homme qu'il me faut' (Piaf-Dumont) were replaced with three more Vaucaire-Dumont compositions: 'Dans leur baiser', 'Marie-Trottoir' and 'Des histoires'. Eight of the nine songs that made it to the album had melodies by Dumont. Basing her comeback on so much new material by just one composer was bold. It meant gambling on her audience's compliance and leaving her comfort zone. But it was essential to the new narrative trope she'd developed: rebirth.

A few days into the run, a TV interviewer commented that her new set had 'another dimension', something that hadn't been there in past shows. She concurred: 'Non, je ne regrette rien', she said, had been a revelation: 'I felt I needed to wipe the slate clean, start all over again, try something totally new. And, mainly in the music of Charles Dumont, I found what I was looking for, a composer who really did help me do something totally new' and who had inspired her regular lyricists to also take 'a new direction, which I think suits me much more than before'.[2] Another leitmotiv of the rebirth trope was a more dramatic contrast between physical appearance and vocal delivery. With her accompanists obscured behind the tulle curtain at her insistence, she made sure she looked alone, tiny and forlorn in that old-fashioned black dress, even a little nervous. But from that body so plainly diminished by illness, the voice dramatically bursts forth as potent and muscular as ever and she knows exactly how to use it to extract maximum emotion from the contrast. As one observer wrote: 'The voice swells, breaking painfully between the two syllables of the verb *aimer*. Loving, love. Words of torment which are the keywords of her success, her power to bewitch.'[3]

The amount of artifice in all this semiology is hard to measure accurately but it's undoubtedly there. Doudou Morizot witnessed a nightly transformation: 'Whereas five minutes before, in the wings, she'd be laughing and joking like a kid, at the top of her voice, on stage she'd become the embodiment of tragedy, Our Lady of Sorrows kind of thing, and people would get taken in every time.'[4] On the opening night, she appeared to forget the words of one of the new songs, 'Mon vieux Lucien'. She interrupted the band and, in her best Parisian street accent rather than the careful diction she used to introduce each song, acknowledged the slip with the easy charm of a pro: 'Y'know what? I got it wrong yesterday too [at the Versailles preview]! I'm gonna start again. I gotta get over this, else I'll never sing it again!'[5] The audience were thrilled at the complicity and applauded graciously. Was this really a second stumble, or a confected piece of theatre after its positive effect the previous night? Some close to the event, including Coquatrix,[6] think it was the latter, although she still got the words slightly wrong when she started again but this time without admitting it. Either way, Pathé wanted to edit out the error but Piaf refused point blank. A wise move, as record buyers would often ask for 'the one where Piaf got it wrong' and sales rocketed accordingly.

The Olympia triumph owed a good deal to stagecraft like this. After a lifetime of self-invention, Édith was skilled at working the crowd and she'd been carefully preparing the rebirth narrative in the run-up to the show. Only weeks after rumours she was finished, she was putting herself about in the media professing excitement about the coming first night. Coquatrix once commented that only the premieres, where all the media and rival artists were present, mattered to her; and she communicated this effectively to the press.[7] 'I just love premieres.… You go out on the stage like it was a lion's cage. You absolutely have to tame them but it's great.… You need these first nights to surpass yourself. Otherwise with the daily grind you'd just fall asleep.'[8]

Her appearance on *Cinq colonnes à la une* on 2 December 1960 was especially important for setting up the comeback. There's a haunting vacancy in her eyes, huge against her white face as she stares blankly into the camera, answering Desgraupes's questions like an automaton. When he says that last winter people had reported her death, she barely reacts, just quietly observing that she didn't know. But she warms up once they move on to the upcoming premiere. Disingenuously given her known drug use, Desgraupes remarks that it's as if she's been injected with something when she starts to sing. This gives her a chance for some industrious self-presentation: I'm not afraid of death; love and song are indivisible; I'm indifferent to wealth; I'm nervous about going back on stage; I go into a trance when I sing, and so on. She then drives all this home with an artful rendition of 'Non, je ne regrette rien'.

Those witnessing or reporting on the first night easily picked up the rebirth theme and the body/voice rhetoric, amenably dramatizing the comeback as an epic struggle between weakness and strength, life and death, defeat and glory. Watching from the wings, the press photographer Hugues Vassal would later give an account of that night in almost ontological terms. She walks on stage before curtain-up looking like a ghost, her hands trembling. Then the miracle occurs:

> What happens next is something like alchemy of the most astonishing kind: a spirit fills the hall, a palpable echo of the amazing exchange which is established in Édith and in the audience, a precious moment which transfigures

the artist, the men and the women [in the audience], who are all suddenly relieved of the superfluous in favour of the essential. Life in its natural state. Emotion at its purest. There's no magic here: only grace. [9]

Vassal also recalls 'the spontaneous undulations of her body, the intuitive movements of her arms and hands [which] accompany and reinforce the expressiveness of her voice'.[10] Much of the writing about the recital displays a similar fascination with her body. This had been a disturbing aspect of reviews since the start of her career, often from the perspective of a misogynistic male gaze. But it had got much worse during the Occupation, after she'd appeared in the film *Montmartre-sur-Seine* in 1941. One male critic on a pro-Nazi newspaper uncompromisingly called her a 'freak', with her 'sickly' appearance, 'hollow eyes and weirdly large head sunk into hunched shoulders'.[11] But a different kind of focus on her body, part pity part morbid curiosity, developed in the 1950s once she began to be ill. Commentators occasionally resorted to medical imagery in search of a dubious witticism: she has been brought from her sick bed by 'a transfusion of songs', chuckled one.[12] But primarily, and almost as a matter of course, they evoked her body and her voice by drawing on the lexis of Christian theology: worship, crucifixion, regeneration and miracle. 'Everything here [in Piaf's flat] is arranged for the celebration of a cult', wrote one reviewer, Michèle Manceaux, admitting that 'religious comparisons come naturally when you write about her.'[13] Manceaux was present at both the Versailles preview and the Olympia first night, in the audience or behind the scenes, and she interviewed Piaf in her flat after the first night; so her lengthy testimony is particularly revealing. She describes 'a little scrap of a woman, deformed like a vine stock by relentless rheumatism', barely able to walk, shoulder blades sticking out 'tragically' from under her blue sweater, yet still with a voice like an organ that 'could fill cathedrals'. The 'religious comparisons' then come thick and fast. 'Last night, Piaf tasted the delights of beatification. Raised from the dead, miraculously cured, Édith, whom the faithful beseech and glorify. Édith as Mary Magdalene', a 'repentant Mary Magdalene, who offers her life, her faith and her loves to her songs'. Mary Magdalene, yes, but also a hint of the Virgin Mary and, just visible between the lines, a female Christ. 'She wants to be the scapegoat, the representative of humanity in all its suffering, the friendly heart of all broken hearts.'[14] Critic after critic is drawn to the same analogies. 'Since 29 December last, the date of the on-stage resurrection of this "heroic little scrap of a woman", the Piaf miracle has been working flat out', wrote one.[15] And another: 'It wasn't a miraculously cured woman they were acclaiming, it was the miracle.'[16] Claude Sarraute wrote in *Le Monde*: 'It's more than a comeback, it's a resurrection. ... Her acting seems sparer, her gestures rarer and so all the more necessary, her voice – that voice that could shatter every microphone, hoarse, vast, desperate – has taken on an unaccustomed gentleness.'[17] Yet another critic begins his review: 'She's there, at the edge of the stage, scrawny and pitiful, crushed by every form of suffering, heart-rending. And then she sings. And it's almost painful that from this body, damaged, worn down, trembling, can issue this huge voice. Like a cry, a long cry, laden with all the serenity in the world.'[18]

This gets to the heart of the fascination with her body. Her voice – 'the seen voice' as it's been called[19] – is incarnate in her physical ruin but transcends it. Is this fascination gendered? Yes, in that it comes close at times to a kind of body-shaming, a voyeuristic, pseudo-medical dissection of her physical disgrace as a woman, and perhaps a furtive desire to watch her die on stage. But what ultimately lifts her out of the intrusive hospital melodrama into the higher realm of tragedy is again that transcendent voice, which spoke to those present on 29 December of female invincibility in terms of messianic resurrection.[20]

# The meanings of the venue

For Doudou Morizot, Piaf was 'the soul' of the Olympia; it 'belonged' to her.[21] Certainly, their destinies were interwoven. Her personal meanings are enmeshed with its history and the meanings of both are bound up with the distinctive evolution of French popular music. By 1960, the Olympia had become an institution, a kind of popular-music conservatoire.[22] It was a rite of passage for any performer seeking consecration and its front rows were coveted by any celebrity or aspirational Parisian wanting to be noticed at first nights. Like Piaf, it had acquired meanings beyond itself and, even at this late stage in her career, she was gilded by it as well as gilding it.

Music halls began to replace the old *cafés-concerts* in France in the 1890s. Situated on the Boulevard des Capucines in the ninth *arrondissement*, the Olympia had existed under that name since 1893 and became one of the great halls of Europe. The famous La Goulue painted by Toulouse-Lautrec performed there. Édith's mother Line Marsa is thought to have sung there in 1927.[23] Initially, it was known for its jugglers, acrobats, mind readers, ventriloquists and a little striptease, with only a sprinkling of singers.[24] Then, in the 1910s, like its rivals the Casino de Paris and the Folies-Bergère, it gained a reputation for the sumptuous revues which made the myth of

Paris by night. Usually divided into loosely connected scenes or tableaux, revues featured lavish visual spectacle, a large cast, sequins and feathers on topless dancing girls, musical comedy acts like the young Maurice Chevalier, a sizeable orchestra and, from 1917 when the Americans joined the war, jazz. For a while, this recipe dominated the Paris halls, sidelining the singing act, or *tour de chant*.[25] But with the hardships of the Great War, shows were forced to focus more on singers, who were cheaper to produce and could serve as a headline act (*meneur* or *meneuse de revue*) linking the various tableaux. In the end, revues came to be identified with these emblematic figures, who went on to be solo singers in their own right, among them Mistinguett, Chevalier, Tino Rossi and Josephine Baker.[26]

In the 1930s, Piaf would benefit from this shift away from revue and become a blueprint for the solo *chanteuse*. With her plain black dress, plaintive voice and economy of gesture, she replaced the sensuous glamour of the revue with a subdued stage identity based initially on the tear-stained melodramas of singers like Fréhel and Marie Dubas, the so-called *chanteuses réalistes* (female realist singers). *La chanson réaliste*, close to the torch song, followed a simple gendered code. Young working-class women, sometimes sex workers or just down on their luck, longing for true love, are invariably crushed by 'misfortune' or 'destiny', though these abstract forces usually come down to a dominant, heartless male. Piaf's physical appearance and the circumstances of her young life slotted easily into this code, which would haunt her career even when she tried to break free of it. It's still explicit in the late portrait of her by an American lover, Doug Davis, which appears on the cover of the album and this book. But she did reinvent it.

The coming of silent cinema after the Great War, followed by talkies, radio and records, caused many music halls to be repurposed as cinemas, including the Olympia in 1929. It wasn't until 1954 that its original vocation was restored by Bruno Coquatrix, whose name it now bears. Under his management, it established its reputation as the 'temple' of variety: 'a kind of sacred site where reputations are made or unmade.'[27] For Coquatrix – musician, songwriter, entrepreneur and briefly the impresario of a very young Édith – reviving the Olympia was costly and balancing its books a constant challenge. For a three-weekly programme, he would hire half a dozen variety turns and up to four singing acts.[28] It was there that many of the future stars of *la chanson française* made their names, among them Gilbert Bécaud, Georges Brassens, Jacques Brel and Juliette Gréco. But Coquatrix also needed established crowd-pleasers to boost the finances, so he cast a wide net to catch big international names: Amália Rodrigues, Lena Horne, Marlene Dietrich, Billie Holiday, Billy Eckstine, Louis Armstrong. And he turned repeatedly to Piaf because she offered the best of both worlds: home-grown icon and international celebrity.

She made her debut there in January 1955 and was booked again in May 1956, after an absence of over fourteen months touring her 'continental revue' in North and South America, including New York's Carnegie Hall. This was a long time to be away and she wasn't quite sure she belonged any more. 'I was afraid, … . It was Paris that mattered, it was Paris I had to win over. And it seemed to me that lots of things had changed. There were new songs, new stars. Was I going to find my way round in all of that?'[29] She needn't have worried. The 1956 show was a triumph and saved the Olympia from closing after only two years. Later that year, she was off to the Americas again, for almost twelve months this time, including a second sell-out booking at Carnegie Hall. Back in France by August 1957, she enjoyed her third triumph at the Olympia in February 1958, where she clocked up a record 128 performances in eight weeks, including three shows on Sundays. She sang before a total of 240,000 and was twice taken ill on stage. The venue too was ailing. By the end of the decade, it was facing bankruptcy again and Coquatrix turned to her to save it once more. Barrier said no until she was offered that fateful song of defiance 'Non, je ne regrette rien' and she left him no choice. Coquatrix would later admit that she saved him and the Olympia from ruin,[30] saving her own finances in the process, their fates still intertwined. At least for now.

Just as her health was failing, the French music scene was changing. As we saw earlier, her final booking by Coquatrix in the autumn of 1962 wasn't always well received. Symbolically, it was immediately followed by the triumphant return of France's nineteen-year-old rock idol, Johnny Hallyday. His admission to this bastion of variety was prognostic. On 20 September 1960, just three months before Piaf's comeback, he'd been included in the first half of an otherwise-standard variety show at a rival music hall, the Alhambra, starring the entertainer Raymond Devos. Johnny's manager claims he'd tried the Olympia but had been given short shrift by Coquatrix.[31] Boldly advertised in the Alhambra programme as 'the prince of rock'n'roll', Johnny, in a tight lace and lamé shirt, performed his trademark trick of rolling on the ground while playing the guitar. One of his biographers maintains that this was the moment French music hall died.[32] Excessive perhaps, but there was certainly uproar, as those in the expensive seats jeered while his young fans standing in the cheaper balcony applauded wildly. Reviewers dismissed him as a hysteric who ought to be consigned to an asylum. But rock wouldn't go away. On 24 February 1961, while Piaf's Olympia show was still running, France's first rock'n'roll festival took place at the enormous Palais des Sports stadium, featuring not only Hallyday and other French rockers but well-known acts from the United States and the United Kingdom. This and a follow-up in June brought the new music to public attention as a dangerous social phenomenon associated with noise, teenage hysteria and delinquency. When Johnny was signed to Philips that August, Jacques Canetti, pioneering producer and seminal promoter of so many chanson careers including Piaf's, promptly resigned. Coquatrix, on the other hand, booked him for the following month.

Such reactions to the advent of rock'n'roll provide a snapshot of a culture on the brink of change from a French popular tradition to American-style showbiz. Although for his first Olympia Johnny donned a tuxedo and had already moved on to the vanilla sounds of the twist, his booking was a sign that the Olympia was bending to the inevitable. Even before 1960, Coquatrix had booked explosive pre-rock acts like Bécaud ('Mr 100,000 Volts') and Sidney Bechet, who had attracted young, over-excited and sometimes destructive audiences. In 1956, he joined forces with the recently created private radio station Europe no. 1 and the French record company Barclay to launch the weekly radio show *Musicorama*. This initially offered Barclay's new signings the chance to do one or two shows at the Olympia when the theatre wasn't booked, which were broadcast on the radio station. But it also opened the way to rock'n'roll: Bill Haley in 1958, Gene Vincent the year after. In June 1963, as Piaf was dying, *Musicorama* introduced a stunned audience to Jerry Lee Lewis whose rendition of 'Good Golly Miss Molly' was described as 'unimaginable, Dantesque, volcanic, reaching unparalleled heights of savagery.'[33] This said it all. Sustained by the Olympia, chanson in the 1950s generally blended tuneful melodies with increasingly thoughtful lyrics in French. Rock was about sound and fury, adolescent eroticism and American dreams. By opening up to it, Coquatrix and his right-hand man Jean-Michel Boris were making a pact with the devil which might just have exacerbated his financial problems. But they were also mapping out the Olympia's future. Three months after Piaf's death, the Beatles were top of the bill.

With hindsight, then, Piaf's return to the Olympia looks defensive. Might it be that the audience's emotional responses to it testified to a burgeoning culture war: an anxious intuition, exacerbated by the Olympia's new programming strategy, that the 'Anglo-Saxon' hordes were at the gates,[34] a pre-emptive nostalgia for a national cultural tradition which, like Piaf herself, was still standing but not in the best of health? I suspect so and I'll come back to this in Chapter 5. But first we need to situate this cultural anxiety against the seismic ideological conflicts that were challenging France's domestic stability and its place in the world, at the very moment Piaf stepped on to the stage in December1960. Conflicts that may look like background but might at some deeper level be foreground.

# Political meanings

Although you'd never guess from her own accounts, the comeback took place at a time of extraordinary historical drama: regime change and fears of a military coup, colonial conflict, torture and terrorism. After the swift fall of France in 1940 and its liberation from Nazi occupation four years later, demands for a similar emancipation intensified in countries under French colonial rule. This led to a second ignominious defeat for the French army at Dien Bien Phu in 1954 and the loss of France's territories in Indochina, immediately followed by another war of independence, this time with Algeria. Although in 1956 France was ready to hand back Tunisia and Morocco, Algeria was a case apart because of its sizeable European population hostile to independence. In metropolitan France too, many in the military were determined not to suffer a third humiliation. As a result, the Algerian war became distinctively savage and divisive. The situation was made all the more intractable by the Fourth Republic's parliamentary system, which led to ineffective coalitions that fell with predictable regularity. Things came to a head in 1958. As Édith was completing her 128 exhausting shows at the Olympia that spring, France was edging closer to civil war. In a neat synchronicity, on 28 April she collapsed on stage in Stockholm just as another French government collapsed in Paris. On 13 May, the army refused to recognize a newly appointed prime minister, Pierre Pflimlin, and backed an uprising of Europeans in Algiers. At this point, there were genuine fears of colonial forces landing in Paris to effect a military takeover like Spain's twenty years before. To some in the army high command, the only way of keeping Algeria French was for the retired General de Gaulle, deemed to have saved the nation during the Occupation, to do so again. Prime minister Pflimlin duly resigned after only a fortnight and de Gaulle agreed to take his place. But with conditions. To guarantee stability, he insisted on having plenary powers for the next six months and on drafting a new constitution that would shift executive power from parliament to an empowered presidency. Despite opposition from the Left, de Gaulle's constitutional revolution was overwhelmingly approved by referendum and he became the first president of the Fifth Republic.

The rebel generals in Algiers assumed he would take their side. But on 8 January 1961, a week or so into Piaf's Olympia booking, another referendum voted in favour of de Gaulle's proposal to offer Algeria self-determination. This led to the formation of the clandestine paramilitary organization the OAS, which made several attempts on de Gaulle's life. On 22 April, not long after her engagement had ended, a military putsch was launched by four retired generals. The First Parachute Regiment (the 1st REP) of the Foreign Legion, stationed in Algeria, spearheaded the operation, seizing vantage points in Algiers. The putsch failed, its leaders were imprisoned and the 1st REP was dissolved. The new president even had to be persuaded not to disband the Legion altogether.

So what was the impact of all these convulsions on Piaf? Ostensibly none at all. Stately as a galleon, her career and personal life cruised through the nation's nervous breakdown without a sideways glance. Yet the meanings attributed to her comeback were still, I suggest, impregnated with it in ways that aren't always obvious or empirically verifiable. One deceptively simple sign was that when the putsch collapsed and the 1st REP left barracks en route for retribution, the song its soldiers sang was an adapted version of 'Non, je ne regrette rien'. The original has remained a Legion favourite ever since, so it has unintentionally retained this distant echo of the Algerian war. But why would the Legion choose that particular song rather than a more historically validated one? One reason is that the army had distributed transistor radios to troops stationed in Algeria and the song was by then a big hit. Another is that it was apparently dedicated to the Legion by Piaf herself.[35] But a third reason has to be the accommodating nature of the lyric. Like many of the best-loved anthems, its defiant words and steady marching beat lend it to appropriation by anyone feeling heroically aggrieved, as we'll see in Chapter 4.

But Piaf's associations with the Legion weren't new or contingent. As an unknown street singer still in her teens, she performed regularly in different barracks on the Paris outskirts. A number of her earliest songs also dramatized the lives of common soldiers, sailors and particularly legionnaires: 'Mon amant de la Coloniale' (My lover in the colonial army), 'Le Fanion de la légion' (The flag of the Legion) and 'Mon légionnaire' (My legionnaire). The ribbon insignia of the Legion was placed on her coffin before burial.[36] For the fiftieth anniversary of her death in 2013, the Legion's band took part in a tribute show, playing both 'Mon légionnaire' and 'Non, je ne regrette rien'.[37] Sentimental militarism was in fact a trope of the imagined Piaf. During the war, she wrote a rousing march called 'Où sont-ils, tous mes copains' (Where are all my pals?), about working-class Frenchmen going cheerily off to war. Despite suspicions of her fraternizing with the Germans, resentment of her tours of POW camps in Germany and a summons to appear before a Resistance purge committee (which quickly exonerated her), she emerged from the war the people's heroine, embodiment of France's irrepressible spirit under occupation, the French Vera Lynn. This image would accompany her right up to her death. In the UK, Vera Lynn's songs of course took much of their connotative power from the war. Less obviously perhaps, Piaf's new 1960 repertoire arguably did the same during the Algerian conflict. Her first night on 29 December was in aid of the highly decorated wartime First Division of the Free French. On 25 September 1962, she sang 'Non, je ne regrette rien' (and other songs) from a platform of the Eiffel Tower for the world premiere of the Normandy landings blockbuster *The Longest Day*, before a 2,700-strong audience of film stars, military personnel, politicians and royalty.

At a no doubt subliminal level, then, the miracle of her resurrection in December 1960 must have felt like a brief moment of national reassurance, the ecstatic responses to it perhaps expressing an unformulated gratitude in the face of Americanization, imperial collapse and a constitutional transformation that broke with almost a century of republican tradition. To say nothing of the global tensions of the Cold War: the Berlin Wall would go up in a matter of months. The fact that this artist, so evocative of a pre-war and wartime France, had now resisted death's dominion offered a metaphor of French exceptionalism, of an untouchable collective soul that, as the world was going mad, was neither defeated nor altered. Straight after the Occupation, Piaf became a vector of therapeutic memory, signifying a nostalgic illusion that France's pre-war self had come through unscathed and pointing the way to national convalescence.[38] I suspect she fulfilled that function again in 1960. The year before, amid constitutional and colonial eruptions, an otherwise trivial showbiz column came up with a sentimental but revealing analogy: 'Just like France, especially last year [during the political crisis of 1958], she was seriously ill. Both seemed condemned. And, just like France, Édith Piaf is now smiling again.'[39] The start of the 1960s was a moment that called for totems of national survival and identity, both political and artistic. Piaf became an emblem of cultural invincibility just as the new president embodied political invincibility. Like Churchill and Vera Lynn in the UK, both were gilded by public memory but purportedly stood aloof from the ideological fray. She may have symbolized rebellion for the Legion but for the wider public it was the opposite: she was a symbol of restored unity in a time of division, a unity made palpable by the shared collective emotion of her comeback. She had been restored to life, just as the new president had risen again to save the nation. Charles de Gaulle and Édith Piaf: twin icons of a new republic.

# **3**   The Record (1)

After the Olympia run, Piaf launched into an unprecedented number of studio sessions. The recordings included 'Mon vieux Lucien', 'Dans leur baiser' and 'Marie-Trottoir', all Dumont melodies she'd used in the show, and the English versions of 'Non, je ne regrette rien' ('No Regrets', lyric by Hal David) and 'Mon Dieu' ('My God', lyric by Yann Dallas). She also recorded the duet 'Les Amants' with Dumont which sets her lyric to his melody, one of her better known late releases. The Olympia triumph and the album's flourishing sales no doubt encouraged this burst of recording, but a question still arises. Was she ever really, even at this late stage, a recording artist in the sense we understand it today, bearing in mind she's always thought of as the archetypal live performer? I want to explore this issue a little further before we look at the album itself.

## **Piaf and recording**

When the industrialization of recording began at the end of the nineteenth century, Pathé became France's first major label but soon lost out to British and American competition. It was bought up in 1928 by the then British label Columbia which, on merging with Gramophone-HMV, became the multinational EMI in 1931. Further concentration produced EMI-Pathé-Marconi in 1936,[1] which included the Columbia France label on which *Récital 1961* would eventually be released. In the 1930s when Piaf's career began, electrical recording, radio, cinema and the microphone were mechanizing the artisanal live landscape she'd grown up with. She worked with these new technologies from the start and her output on disc is substantial.

Of the 500 or so songs she performed over the years, she recorded around 400, not all of them released at the time.[2] When she first went into the studio, in 1935, sound reproduction was becoming more sophisticated, new professions were emerging like sound engineer and 'artistic director' (*directeur artistique*),[3] and supply and demand were expanding as labels scouted for new talent. But it was radio that gave her a way in to that new environment. Jacques Canetti, artistic director at Polydor, a subsidiary of Deutsche Grammophon, was also in charge of programming at the private radio station Radio-Cité. As soon as he heard Piaf, he got her to perform on the station's Sunday morning show for new talents. Radio was a more democratic medium than records in those days: fewer than 5 per cent of French homes owned gramophones,[4] which perhaps explains Polydor's curious marketing slogan: 'the record for the elite'. She was an instant hit with listeners and Canetti signed her to record four songs that December, released on 78rpm the following spring, still under the name Louis Leplée had given her, 'La Môme Piaf'.[5] That same month, she made her first film appearance, in *La Garçonne* (The tomboy). She stayed at Polydor until 1945, when it could no longer finance the large orchestra she now insisted on recording with. Pathé-Marconi was altogether more attractive, with studios in Paris and an extensive pressing plant in Chatou. So she joined many other French singers on its Columbia label, where she stayed until her death, apart from a brief spell with Decca (1947–8).

In one sense, then, she and her contemporary Charles Trenet (on Pathé, then Columbia) were the first stars of a French record industry. Yet in her case, the picture is more complicated. Due to slow economic recovery after the war, France lagged behind the States in moving from the shellac 78rpm to vinyl.[6] Piaf herself didn't make the switch until around 1955,[7] so she actually released very few studio albums in her lifetime once vinyl made the long player possible. One artistic director at Columbia, Pierre Hiégel, recalls that she much preferred to record on stage, hating studio sessions.[8] When they couldn't be avoided, she would approach them as live performances, rehearsing at home, learning songs by heart and perfecting an act for each. The orchestra, usually Robert Chauvigny's, would stand and applaud as she came in. She would insist on singing the entire song through, with no interruptions from sound engineer or producer, from whom any tremulous suggestions were abruptly dismissed anyway. She might at this stage change a word in a song or an instrument that didn't sound right. Certainly, she was a perfectionist in the studio and was always willing to do more takes, but invariably the later ones lacked the spontaneity of the first.[9] So the live album was her natural medium, capturing her at her most performative and powerful.

But isn't a recording of a live show a second best: neither a meticulously crafted studio artefact nor the full sensuous experience of the original spectacle? Not in Piaf's case. It's been argued that the recorded voice generally gives more intimate, more authentic access to the actual body of the singer than a live performance alone where visual distractions and pre-existing media images as it were intrude and where in any case the spectator is often at a distance from the stage.[10] But of Piaf specifically, the chanson theorist Stéphane Hirschi maintains that her decisive contribution to the genre is in fact her ability, unlike other realist singers, to embody all the physicality of live performance in her voice and therefore on record, allowing us to visualize her stage presence, to hear her body in her voice.[11] Certainly, Piaf's body is audible on *Récital 1961* in various subtle ways: in her impeccable articulation, in the throaty rawness of the low notes and the slightly metallic edge in some of the higher or louder ones, and in the way her voice occasionally has to slide up to hit the right note. But we can hear it most of all in what linguists call the apical trill. When she sings words containing the letter *r*, the tip of her tongue often vibrates several times against the alveolar ridge just behind the teeth, rather than at the back of the throat where in everyday speech the more standard Parisian /R/ (also known as a uvular fricative), is formed.[12] In 'Non, je ne regrette rien', for example, when she announces the song's title, she uses the Parisian /R/, but as soon as she sings 'rien de rien', the tip of her tongue becomes audible, as it also does on 'regrette' or later on the word 'trémolo'. In 'Les Flonflons du bal', it's easily heard on 'tourner' and 'triple'. As the Parisian /R/ has become standard in most of France, this apical variant is now heard as a stylized, theatrical form of delivery, also used by classical actors. By adopting it with such insistence, Piaf implicitly endows the popular song with a legacy, an historical legitimacy.

Another way of thinking about the live album is the idea that recording has brought about a fundamental transformation of song by producing what Hirschi describes enigmatically as a 'controlled fleetingness'.[13] The centuries-old practice of singing a newly written lyric to an existing tune in the public domain (known as *un timbre* in French), so that words and music existed as separate interchangeable components, was revolutionized by the advent of the phonograph, which changed the song from a practice into a form, a finite product limited to three minutes by the 78rpm format, words and music now joined in an indivisible whole. By the same token, a one-off, ephemeral performance of a song, by a particular singer with a particular accompaniment in a particular time and place, became 'fixed', to use Hirschi's word. Infinitely reproducible and with all listeners to that recording hearing the same performance, it was a work rather than a practice, and even, potentially, a work of art.[14]

Music theorists have also observed that records transform *how* we listen. Antoine Hennion calls this discomorphosis, because recording makes possible a familiarity and an intimacy with a piece of music unimaginable in the past.[15] If we extrapolate from both these theories, we can better understand the nature of *Récital 1961*. The recording of a live performance places it in a liminal dimension between ephemerality and permanence, practice and product. A unique, irretrievable moment – each show different from the previous night's and performed in front of a different audience, who would normally hear it only once – becomes calcified like the inhabitants of Pompeii in a fleeting posture. This gives us the chance to appreciate and even study one night's performance at the Olympia sixty years after it happened, in the edited, self-contained and infinitely reproducible form of a record. The living, breathing, fallible Piaf – that quintessentially live performer who sang in person everywhere from the Paris streets to Carnegie Hall, whose voice could vary from one night to the next, and who could get a lyric wrong in the heat of the moment – is caught and bottled forever. Her performance that night is no longer a point in time but a work we can listen to on repeat, each successive listening shaped by all our previous ones. She must have instinctively known this. She tightly controlled the production of the album, choosing the songs to be included, overriding the producer Jacques Poisson's preference for more of them, selecting the portrait of her that appears on the cover.[16] She was furious when Poisson edited out the mistake she'd made on 'Mon vieux Lucien', insisting it be restored for the sake of authenticity.

The full recording of the show was finally edited down to just nine tracks, five on side 1, four on side 2. As we know, all the melodies bar one are by Dumont, three of the lyrics are by Rivgauche, four by Vaucaire and two by Piaf herself. The centrepiece is clearly the big comeback number, 'Non, je ne regrette rien', though its positioning on the record wouldn't suggest as much. It would have made a rousing closing track but it comes second on side 2 and seventh overall. So, we have to wonder whether there's actually a logic to the running order, a shape or thematic coherence. I suspect there is. Piaf seems to have understood that a live LP gives privileged access that the audience at the time didn't have. It can produce new meanings, new readings of the songs and of the album as a whole. The iconography of the sleeve alone is revealing. Doug Davis's empathetic interpretation of her, which occupies the whole front cover with no intrusive titling or other wording, recalls her past as a *chanteuse réaliste* but also the dominant narrative of her life since then: the tortured but beautiful face, the drooping eyes half-closed with pain, the tiny body leaning forward in supplication, the defeated tilt of the exaggeratedly large head with the left shoulder raised to support it, as if she can no longer hold it high, or just for a little bodily warmth; and, within all this, a distant reminiscence of Christ dead on the cross. The songs chime with that visual narrative up to a point, yet they are also autobiographical in rather different, more complex ways, which amount to a new staging of the imagined Piaf that sits in discreet tension with the cover. It's those different, complex ways I want to explore track by track in this and the next chapter, the record allowing us to read the songs and their internal relationships more closely.

# Side 1

## *Track 1: 'Les Mots d'amour' (Words of love), Rivgauche-Dumont (pp.305–7)*

This opener isn't one of her best-known songs, but it is one of her most thought-provoking.[17] Recorded in November 1960 and released on the same EP as 'Non, je ne regrette rien',[18] it was another song she had trouble learning, stumbling over it in Rheims when she was trying out the new set. At the Olympia, she was word-perfect.

Rivgauche was always one of her more reflective writers and the tale his lyric tells here differs from what we're first led to expect. The track begins with a gentle lilt and a deceptively familiar motif. A first-person narrator is emoting breathlessly in love-song clichés. I've never loved as madly as this, I want to shout it from the rooftops, I'd die if you ever left me, and so on. The wording of each declaration is half-repeated in the next, as if the sentiments were tumbling out, unstoppable and disordered. There's the same urgency in Piaf's delivery, reinforced by the need to elide seven or eight syllables into the six notes available in each melodic line, so that, for example, the two syllables of 'je peux' (I can) become one: 'j'peux'. Marc Bonel's accordion underscores the effect by slightly accelerating the tempo and volume towards the end of each short line, discreetly disrupting the usually reassuring java tempo.

After this febrile opening stanza, which actually turns out to be the chorus, the first verse brings us down to earth. We've probably assumed that the person speaking was a woman, as she is voiced by Piaf. And we know from the masculine pronoun at the start of verse 1 that her lover is a man. But we now discover that the words of love were his, not hers, and that she was reporting them with bitterness. For the only truly 'mad' thing about their relationship is that, having spoken of his love with so much passion, he just walked out on her. Disenchantment is now emphasized by the sentimental string accompaniment that joins the accordion in this verse. Because, of course, he didn't die without her as he promised he would. But then neither did she.

A musical full-stop at the end of verse 1 creates a pause for sad reflection, before an exact repeat of the chorus, though by this stage the narrator is already sounding a trifle weary. Verse 2 reveals why. For she herself is now repeating those self-same words of love to another man, and with exactly the same passion as her ex once evinced with her. The hollowness of the words, however, is now acknowledged, for in the rendition captured on the album but also in the studio recording, Piaf abandons the printed lyric halfway through a line and fills in with two 'la-la-la', which have all the weight of blah blah blah. Verse 3 then drives home a brutal truth. The clichéd words of love were not actually being spoken by any of the characters involved. They were speaking themselves. This is what words of love do: they run away with us. As the lyric puts it, it's the 'voice of love' saying them, mechanically, like a record. No wonder, then, that in the final chorus, where she's now telling yet another man how madly she loves him like she never has before, she rattles off an abbreviated version of each cliché, placing the same bored emphasis on the last word of each line. And yet she ends the song with a rising inflexion on 'love', underscored by lush, emotional strings. Rivgauche has cleverly scripted a final sad irony here by qualifying 'aimer' with 'd'amour', a locution used in French to distinguish liking from full-on loving. Maybe the earlier relationships failed because they were just about *aimer*, whereas this time, at long last, it really is true love, *aimer d'amour*. But no one is fooled. Piaf expertly performs a musical wink by pausing briefly between 'aimer' and 'd'amour' (indicated by ellipsis in the printed text[19]) and her voice slides wearily up to the final high note rather than hitting it triumphantly. She makes sure we get the irony.

The song nicely illustrates what Barthes calls a lover's discourse: the 'repertoire' or 'thesaurus' that makes up the language of love.[20] Through repetition, inflexion and tempo, Piaf highlights the distance between the lexical codes that desire induces the lover to employ and the harsh realities of relationships. The problem with words of love is that there are just 'too many of them', the lyric reveals, they are just too available, orbiting round us like a persistent fly regardless of what they, or we, mean. But if that's the case, in what corner of public discourse do they actually reside? Well, in popular songs, of course. This discreet element of meta-chanson, song about song, provides a further layer of signification for the keen listener, as Piaf's delivery subtly deconstructs the sentimental love song she has long been associated with. 'Les Mots d'amour' thus becomes an oblique reflection on her own career. The plaintiveness built into her timbre and skilfully put to work in her phrasing suggests that this really is a song about the aspiration to true love. But that is its tragedy. She expresses not bitterness but the melancholy of knowledge: the knowledge that, to divert Sartre's famous phrase, love is 'a useless passion'. In this respect, 'Les Mots d'amour' has autobiographical baggage for Piaf cognoscenti. It's a post-Cerdan song. As one biographer points out,[21] the title contains an intertextual allusion to Piaf's own lyric for the world-famous 'La Vie en rose' (1945), in which the adored lover says 'words of love' to the narrator that move her.[22] The intertextuality here constructs a before-and-after. Before Cerdan, the imagined Piaf saw life through rose-tinted spectacles. After his death, as the audience knows, there's been nothing but a succession of affairs, each a longed-for potential replacement but none amounting to anything. Hence the nervous rush of her delivery. The febrility in those words of love indicates a desperate attempt at self-hypnosis: with each new affair, she pretends to fall in love again with the passion she once felt for Cerdan. But she never does and never can. His death is both a metaphor and a catalyst of the failure of love.

Even so, there is a kind of uplift in the song, a discreet assertion of female agency. The Piaf it imagines comes out on top simply by virtue of her lucidity. The three implied males in the song are mere shadows; they have no idea of the role they are playing. Only the imagined Piaf knows and understands the real nature of this existentialist drama; only she sees song, love and life for what they are. Like Sisyphus, she keeps rolling the stone back up the hill, knowing she'll have to watch it tumble down again and begin the long hopeless climb once more. But none of this complexity makes the song opaque or unapproachable and it clearly didn't do so on the night. It's just that the reflection made possible by the recording allows us to identify new layers of meaning within it.

## Track 2: 'Les Flonflons du bal' (the blaring sound of dance music), Dumont-Vaucaire (pp.307–8)

This track brings a change of mood and depth. It's one of the Dumont songs she'd turned down a year before, claiming it was so much like a Piaf song that she didn't want it.[23] It's much less complex than 'Les Mots d'amour'. The first-person protagonist hears loud popular music from the street below, presumably from a nearby dance hall (*bal*). Her attic room is in a working-class neighbourhood: the walls are dirty and the music has the brutal carelessness of a street party. This is conveyed by an intro consisting of nerve-jangling brass and percussion with an accordion underlay and the almost oompah-pah style of the 3/4 time signature. Piaf also belts out the vocal at an ear-splitting pitch, with an exhilarating key-change midway and an uplift on the very last notes. So, in purely sonic terms, this is an upbeat number reproducing the dance music she's hearing. But that's where the poignancy lies. All this noise reminds her of her own romantic past but now, although she shuts herself away in her room, the sound of people enjoying themselves exacerbates her pain, since her man, addressed directly as 'you', has gone. Again, the listener can't help but read the singer's own life into the performance. It's said that when she sang the line 'I very nearly died', the audience gasped.[24] Perhaps this was in recognition of Piaf's own near-death experiences but the lyric also invited them to make another connection to the Cerdan story.

Despite the banal lyric, there's again a meta dimension of sorts, though a simpler one. Like a number of her songs, 'Les

Flonflons' is about the negative effects of popular music on emotions. When your heart is broken, joyful music will only intensify your pain. And this song's own relentless joviality joins a string of Piaf classics featuring a manic, almost hallucinatory dancehall or circus: 'Bal dans ma rue' (1949), 'Padam … padam' (1951), 'Bravo pour le clown' (1953), and even to an extent 'Milord' (1958). All of these refer back intertextually to 'L'Accordéoniste' (1942). Here, a former prostitute who loses her accordionist husband in the war is magnetically drawn back to the dance hall where they met and where now, in a wretched pantomime, she dances to the accordion music played by another, until she can stand it no longer and screams for it to stop.

## Track 3: 'T'es l'homme qu'il me faut' (You're the man for me), Piaf-Dumont (pp.314–15)

Although this number was eventually dropped from the show, it reappears on the album. The lyric was written by Piaf herself, so that may be one reason why it does, but it's also load-bearing in the album's overall narrative. On the surface, it's lightweight like 'Les Flonflons', with touches of the novelty song, limp rhymes, love-song clichés and constant repetition. The title is repeated five times, while the shortened 'you're the man' appears thirteen times. The main thing about this man is that he 'never overdoes it', which we're told four times. This is someone who achieves perfection through moderation. He simply doesn't see other women, even though they quite clearly look at him. He likes a laugh but is also serious. He has the knack of personifying love, happy days, light and life, tenderness and caresses. Unusually for a Piaf song, this one has a jaunty, soft rock'n'roll rhythm, with a light electric guitar and a piano riff midway in each verse, typical of the very late 1950s when rock'n'roll was settling into an unthreatening pop idiom. There's an American feel to the sound and, for the British listener, that guitar has the homely amplification of Cliff Richard's 'Summer Holiday'. Piaf's voice sounds more playful too.

But this US-sounding arrangement, together with her witty vocal, actually suggests a less cursory reading. The repetitions contradict the standard rhetoric about the supposedly 'poetic' nature of chanson in that the lyrics make sounds more than sense. And those sounds evoke a lip-smacking and subtly subversive eroticism. In her delivery of her own lyric, she performs a different Piaf. Rather than tragic tales of suffering and victimhood, what we get is much closer to reality. Her avatar in the song has sexual agency rather than being the classically 'realist' female, mortified, victimized, psychologically emaciated. She in fact reverses the Pygmalion myth which had previously been a trope in so many of her songs and in her early life. Men – her father, her managers, her first lovers – had tried to sculpt her into a statue matching their aspirations. But once she became established, she reversed the polarity, setting about micro-managing her own persona and turning her men – sexual partners, husbands, colleagues – into the kind of companions or performers she wanted them to be. This reversal on the threshold of the 1960s informs the song. It challenges the Pygmalion dynamic of male-centred pop songs like Cliff Richard's 'Living Doll' (1959), whose title says it all; or, a little later, the Stones' even less reconstructed 'Under My Thumb' (1966), where the male narrator's troublesome girlfriend has somehow been persuaded to only speak when she's spoken and not to look at other men. In 'T'es l'homme', the Piaf avatar is an experienced assessor of men and has given her latest model a thorough pre-sale inspection. His moderation may make him dull but it also objectifies him. She parades him proprietorially, clutching his arm so other women know whom he belongs to. Piaf's delivery also gets progressively steamier. She relishes his voice and repeatedly orders him to talk, which makes her feel 'so good', said four times followed by a mildly lascivious sigh of pleasure on 'oh yes, really good' (verse 4). Then, after some platitudes about his being the light in her life, we get to the nub of his appeal: that bit about tenderness and caresses. Again, we hear the body in the voice. Her tongue lingers on 'lll'homme' and her lips elongate the *m* in 'mmmoi'. We also hear two chuckles and a raunchy growl. The carnal pleasure the man provides becomes increasingly audible as she builds up to the crescendo consisting of three languorous repeats of 'me too' and a bluesy slide up to pitch on 'I love you'. We might call this oral sex if the phrase hadn't already been taken.

The song ends slightly mystifyingly, when she calls him her 'problem' and says that she doesn't understand because, 'despite all this' (all what?), she loves him 'too', presumably meaning as much as he loves her. The rhythm changes here too, slowing to an insistent soft-rock beat as if to mark that something different is happening. We might suspect that *problème* has been introduced only to set up the closing rhyme with *je t'aime*, but it also makes sense within the reversed Pygmalion logic. Having moulded her dream lover, she has, like Pygmalion, fallen in love with her own creation. Perhaps he's the substitute for Cerdan she could never find. Or perhaps he just is Cerdan. At any event, what comes over with the help of the new melodic opportunities supplied by Dumont is the assertion of female empowerment that we saw in 'Les Mots d'amour'. And also a touch of the same meta awareness. For isn't this impossibly idealized man a composite of those empty love-song clichés that prove so addictive in 'Les Mots d'amour'? Again, nothing in this reading of the song stops it being a light, entertaining piece both musically and lyrically, wildly applauded on the night. It's the magnifying glass proffered by the record that makes the subtext detectable.

## Track 4: 'Mon Dieu' (My God), Vaucaire-Dumont (pp.315–16)

We're in very different territory now. In just three minutes fifty-two seconds, Piaf summons all the kitsch religiosity of the Hollywood biblical epic, making it one of her most revered songs. It's tempting to wonder why, at least on the strength of the lyric alone, which has a revealing back-story. After adopting 'Non, je ne regrette rien', Piaf was keen to know what else Dumont had up his sleeve. He played her another song by Vaucaire and himself, called 'Toulon, Le Havre, Anvers'. She liked the tune but not the words, which drew too much on her realist themes of whores, sailors and ports. In a phone call in the early hours, Vaucaire was instructed to come up with a new lyric by 5pm the same day. The haste of the rewrite shows through if we take the lyric at its most literal. In French, the phrase 'mon Dieu' as used here signifies not the English 'my God', expressing surprise or horror, but a vocative supplication equivalent to 'dear God', or 'Oh Lord'. The first-person narrator is in fact appealing to the divinity to grant her more time with her beloved. Beyond this, we learn next to nothing. The first line consists only of three 'Mon Dieu!', which is eventually uttered eleven times. In chorus 2, she replaces one 'mon Dieu' with 'Oh oui', suggesting ecstatic communion with the Almighty. Yet, looked at dispassionately, her prayer sounds more like impudent horse-trading. She starts the bidding at a very modest one day. Or could we make it two, or maybe a week? In the second chorus, she eccentrically ups her bid to six months but immediately lowers it to three, or two, and eventually one. But what we never find out is why she needs to petition God in the first place. Is her lover threatening to leave? Is he dying? Or might they have only just met, given that she pleads for more time 'to start or finish' and 'make memories together'? In which case, why is she begging for an extra allowance, if the relationship is so new that they haven't had time to find out where it's going?

But such matters of internal logic sound picky if we stop thinking about the lyric in isolation from the music and the imagined Piaf. To really make sense of the song's impact, we have to picture a woman who's been round the block, disappointed many times, and who is now pleading for a relationship to last just for once. Its full emotional impact on the night can then be explained by two overlapping autobiographical narratives. First, thanks to media coverage and her existing repertoire, the audience in 1960 knows (or thinks it knows) the heartbreak caused by her many failed affairs. Then, beneath this first narrative, there's again the inevitable Cerdan myth. This prompts us to ignore the present tense and imagine either a prescient Piaf in 1949, full of foreboding before the air crash, asking for the love of her life not to die, or a 1960 Piaf so traumatized by the memory of that loss that she's unable to believe a new love could ever last. In this way, the song comes to be about emotional insecurity, taking its power from her tragic past: abandoned by her mother, neglected by her father, losing a child, losing Cerdan. And, like 'Hymne à l'amour' which it resembles in its quasi-religious intensity, it's a song about death. Her anxious longing for a little more time serves as a metonym for the hope that her comeback might mark a deferral of her own demise.

Then, of course, there's the music. In the lyric alone, these contextual levels of meaning are present as it were in waiting. They are only bodied forth in performance, in the vocal, melody and arrangement: the sympathetic piano trills, the strings furiously emoting as if in a wartime movie, the celestial backing voices that kick in for the second chorus followed by a single angelic soprano underscoring the triplets of 'my God' in the second verse. And most of all her vocal and visual interpretation. One commentator describes the prayer-like quality of her regular renditions of the song: 'she chants it with her hands open in the posture of the believer who raises her palms up to heaven, then brings them back down, fingers apart … like two great butterflies'.[25] But it's not quite that straightforward. Vocally, she begins in a low, slow pitch that certainly suggests a hymn-like solemnity. But she then delivers the verse's first line, which pleads for time for the lovers to love, with abrupt passion, close to anger or a stamp of the foot. Her voice continues to fluctuate in this way until, underscored by an emphatic drum roll, she finally belts out the reclamatory last word: 'more' (*encore*). This is not a prayer for forgiveness, salvation, or even for moral guidance since she explicitly demands to keep her lover even if she's in the wrong. It's a strictly secular appeal for more time, more life. For her and for all of us. Although there are odd moments when she has to slide up to pitch, as with the first 'amoureux' and 'souvenir', this is a performer at the top of her game, expertly working the crowd, deploying vocal, melody, arrangement and stagecraft to squeeze maximum existential angst from a rather lame lyric.

## Track 5: 'Mon vieux Lucien' (My mate Lucien), Rivgauche-Dumont (pp.308–10)

While Piaf was trialling her Olympia set at a handful of lesser venues, between Rheims and Nancy she asked Dumont and Rivgauche to come up with a song for her chiropractor Lucien Vaimber, whose treatment had helped her get back to performing. This composition was the result. It was also the one she famously got wrong: first in Versailles, having only received the lyrics the day before, then again at the Olympia where she sportingly confessed to the error. Musically, the song resembles earlier upbeat numbers like 'La Goualante du pauvre Jean' (1954) or 'Milord'. Its jaunty style mixes music hall with New Orleans trad jazz. There's a bouncy banjo in the foreground, what sounds like a tuba on beats 1 and 3 in the background, and a honky-tonkish piano towards the end.[26] The vocal is brash and her diction broad and unpolished. All of which illustrates both the class and the character of the male lead, for, unusually for Piaf, the song contains no female narrator. It stages an encounter in Lucien's room with the unnamed speaker, though we only hear the latter's voice. This man, Lucien's friend, is clearly a tiresome practical joker, his latest jape being to have invited their gang of mates over to Lucien's unannounced, 'just for a laugh', although the others haven't arrived yet. No doubt the plan is for them all to go out drinking or whoring. Unduly pleased with himself at having caught Lucien on the hop, his banter continues unremittingly until it finally dawns on him that Lucien hasn't yet spoken. Spotting his friend's puffy eyes, he wonders if he's woken him up but then realizes he's been writing to his girlfriend. At this point he notices something in a drawer that Lucien is trying to conceal and asks what it is. We don't find out but the friend does and for one fleeting moment he's afraid. He quickly regains his composure (or pretends to), assuming that Lucien in turn is having a laugh. Anyone who didn't know you, he crows, would've fallen for your little game, but not me! He's about to leave Lucien to finish the letter but he can't quite bring himself to go, still trying to reassure himself that each is teasing the other. After all, he says with feigned amusement, there's no chance of Lucien of all people suffering from a broken heart. Then, suddenly, things move very fast. As Piaf's band honky-tonks away, Lucien seizes whatever he was hiding and the friend shouts 'What the hell, Lucien!' and orders him to hand it over. Then, 'Oh no, Lucien!'. The song ends, unresolved.

Rivgauche's lyric cleverly draws us into this unfolding drama but leaves the singer to interpret the outcome, which Piaf does very skilfully. The words on the page allow for a cinematic ending where Lucien might grab a gun and shoot himself just as the friend leaps forward to stop him, thereby indicting the friend for his insensitivity. But Piaf's enactment on stage is psychologically subtler: the friend, more annoyed than anything at being forced into an unwanted male intimacy, holds out a peremptory hand for the deadly object, looks at it with brief disgust, then throws it aside.[27] Still with a note of exasperation and sounding like a parent scolding a child, he brusquely cajoles Lucien as if telling him to pull himself together, then in a softer tone of resentful indulgence orders him to come out with his mates as planned.

Piaf's sensitive reading requires all the skill of a stage actor, as the meaning of this pocket drama has to be teased out from an uninterrupted monologue. Wittingly or not, it harks back to Cocteau's play *Le Bel Indifférent*, in which she herself played the monologuing female lead, with her co-star silently reading the paper throughout. As in the play, the dramatic interest of the song lies not in the silent character's heartache but in the finely drawn portrait of the loquacious protagonist. As the happy-go-lucky arrangement and Piaf's brassy delivery suggest, he presents as Jack the Lad but is in reality socially inept, pathetically anxious to establish himself as everyone's favourite joker. No wonder it takes him so excruciatingly long to register the truth. When he spots whatever is in Lucien's drawer, there's a pause in Piaf's delivery and a look of disbelief, as she enacts the friend's laborious efforts to compute what's happening. But he's so out of his depth emotionally, so used to using banter to avoid communication, that he nearly makes the disastrous mistake of leaving Lucien alone. Only at the last minute, when Lucien openly seizes the means of his destruction, does the penny drop. Lucien's motivation at this point is intriguing too. Doesn't he secretly want his friend to understand, to notice his grief in time to stop him, which the friend very nearly fails to do? A comparison with 'Milord' illuminates the point. In both songs it's a man suffering the pains of love. The female voice in 'Milord' is a sex worker, whom we might expect to be inured to the feelings of her punters. But unlike Lucien's pal, she's able to handle the English lord's broken heart with a streetwise intelligence. Even in songs where men ruggedly bond over matters of the heart – Jacques

Brel's 'Jef', for example, or Renaud's 'Manu' – male friends show greater sensitivity than the inadequate dimwit depicted here. Ultimately, 'Mon vieux Lucien' is a song about the reluctance of men to deal with emotion. The musical setting might deceive the casual listener but it's an essential part of understanding the psychological dynamic of the song.

# 4 The Record (2)

## Side 2

### Track 6: 'La Ville inconnue' (Strange city), Vaucaire-Dumont

This is an intriguing song, familiar yet enigmatic.[1] For reasons unexplained, the first-person narrator is wandering the streets of a city she doesn't know. She's detached, almost anomic, adrift on the endless thoroughfares. Cold-shouldered by edgy passers-by, she's afraid of the night but dreads returning to her lonely hotel room, her empty bed and the prospect of waking up to another day. Yet all she really wants is to sleep and remember when she was loved. She thinks about her former lover, wondering if he even remembers her. This is the extent of the story. But story here is less important than atmosphere. Meaning lies in mood. This is generated by visual imagery to an extent – docks, empty boulevards, bare grey walls, a train rattling over a bridge – but above all by melody, instrumentation and vocal, which are resolutely urban and take most of the signifying weight. The song opens with a clash of cymbals, blaring brass and an ominous drum roll, followed by Dany Kane's melancholy blues harmonica, reminiscent of Larry Adler. In between, we hear sleazy brass and woodwind sounding like cacophonous car horns, tinkling late-night jazz piano, and more cymbals. Piaf's vocal matches this with a steely vibrato and by elongating her phrasing with bluesy slides up to pitch. The whole effect is cinematic, inescapably black-and-white. Like French New Wave films of the same period or the slightly earlier picture *Touchez pas au grisbi* (Jacques Becker, 1954),[2] it draws on the noir aesthetic of US crime movies and TV series from the 1940s and 1950s, in the same way as songs like Gene Pitney's 'Town without Pity' for the movie of that name, or parts of the score from *West Side Story*, both from 1961. This is Maigret's Paris, Godard's Alphaville, or a rainy night in Georgia. But with a female lead there's a further menace that recalls the *chanson réaliste*, where vulnerable young women who have experienced loss wander the 'zone', the sinister outskirts of the French capital.[3] There's nothing here to reduce the danger or humanize the streets. They're deserted, unfathomably long and bewildering, possibly even circular. The late-night elevated train has a clear destination, its journey is linear; but hers is endless and aimless as she wanders round 'like a stray dog'. The circularity is finally confirmed by the return of the mournful harmonica at the end. Far beyond the trite love story, this is a song about urban alienation.

## Track 7: 'Non, je ne regrette rien' (No, I regret nothing), Vaucaire-Dumont (pp.287–8)

One of her biggest hits and best-loved international standards even today – the last in fact to be canonized – this song was the centrepiece of both concert and album, not least because it was so heavily publicized as the trigger for her sensational comeback. By June 1961, *Billboard Music Week* was listing the studio version, released on an EP (ESRF1303), as top of its rudimentary French hit parade.[4] On the vinyl re-release of the album for the twentieth anniversary of her death (1983), it was promoted to title track: *Olympia 61 Non, je ne regrette rien*. So its positioning on the original LP, as neither scene-setting intro nor grand finale, may seem odd. But the fact that it comes straight after 'La Ville inconnue' carries meaning.

Dumont imagined the melody as a revolutionary march but Vaucaire struggled to find a suitable lyric and, so the story goes, kept repeating to himself 'no, I won't find anything'. Meanwhile, Piaf had confessed in a recent interview that she regretted nothing about her past and would do it all again, 'second by second'.[5] Eventually, this confession combined with Vaucaire's recurring expression of self-doubt to suggest a title and a subject. Though Dumont wasn't happy with the result, especially the drawn-out 'Non' of the first line,[6] Piaf definitely was.

On the first night, the song is known to the audience as they react enthusiastically as soon as she announces it. As well as the four warm-up shows in December, she had released it on record that same month. Radio listeners might also have heard it in a programme she did for Europe no.1 in November and TV audiences could have discovered it on 2 December in the interview for *Cinq colonnes à la une*. Nonetheless, the Olympia rendition on the 29th was where the song became legend. On the edited record, the rhapsodic applause, which begins even before the orchestra finishes, is allowed to last 43 seconds, punctuated with exclamations and cries for more. Dumont sees the 'miracle' of the song as the way it harmonizes 'a melody full of anger with words of acceptance and hope'.[7] Just as important, though, is the way Vaucaire makes us identify the anger, acceptance and hope as Piaf's own. There's no third party here: narrator and singer are one.

The binaries that sustain the lyric – good and bad, pain and pleasure, experiences not regretted but learnt from – echo the biographical themes that Piaf and the media have been feeding the public for years. To reinforce the identification, Vaucaire uses a conversational idiom. The 'rien de rien' which starts the song (the title of an earlier Piaf song with lyrics by Aznavour) is an informal expression that drops the listener into the middle of a conversation. The protagonist's reply to an unseen questioner more or less means: 'No, not a single solitary thing. Nope, I don't regret a thing.' Then, lest any doubt remain, she adds: 'I couldn't give a shit about the past.' Is this Piaf refusing to be cajoled into remorse by an inquisitive interviewer? Or the mature Piaf telling her younger self to get over herself and move on? I think there's a third reading available, possibly the most important.

Still in conversation mode, the very last line introduces an unidentified 'you' (using the familiar *toi*), conceivably the person asking the question. This is why she has no regrets: she's found happiness with a new love. Gossip columnists speculated whether this 'toi' was Dumont, but he denies they were ever lovers. Nor could it have been her second husband Théo Sarapo as he wasn't yet on the scene. In fact, there seems to have been nobody special in her life at this point, not surprisingly given her failing health. So, isn't this deus ex machina a rather lame dénouement for so powerfully assertive a song, reducing it to just another ditty about finding true love? There's surely more to it than that. Ultimately, the 'you' is us, her public. Her rendition of the song turns it into a statement about her comeback, about a return to life made possible by the audience's willingness to bear witness to her triumph over her body. This is conveyed by voice, arrangement and onstage personation.

The vocal starts on that long 'non' with a proud, throaty vibrato. It then steadily rises with the melody until she perfectly hits the closing high note on 'you', which she holds as the band reaches its own crescendo just behind her. The trotting effect of the 12/8 time in the instrumental introduction also produces anticipation: something great is coming. We might visualize a tired but proud warrior quietly riding home after the battle of a lifetime. Or Piaf as Joan of Arc, Liberty leading the people. In her TV rendition on *Cinq colonnes à la une* in early December 1960, she stands to attention for most of the song, as if for the national anthem, hands pressed to her sides, feet slightly apart, eyes fixed forward and head held high. Apart from a few assertive tosses of the head and an occasionally pointing finger, she remains motionless until the final 'Non, rien de rien'. At this point, she raises her clenched fists and thrusts them down again with petulant refusal and a brief shake of the head. Then, as she begins the closing crescendo and as the strings rise with the vocal, her fists again rise in tandem and cross against her chest, her brow furrowed. On the 'aujourd'hui' (today), she briefly tosses her head with proud conviction and as she reaches the culminating 'you', the fists open and the fingers spread expansively, like two captive birds escaping to freedom.[8] In a slightly later stage version from the Olympia show, once her stage interpretation had evolved, those hands open more expansively in the direction of her enraptured public.[9] The audience instantly explodes, with admiration and gratitude: for being included in the song, for the autobiographical revelation she's just offered them and for the defiance she's stirred within them by reaching out, as a perceptive biographer puts it, to 'those who felt, or thought they felt, the same way, and more particularly those who wished they dared to'.[10]

This is a song that inspires and consoles. Like the defeated legionnaires in Algiers, anyone can use it to drape their own resentments, disappointments or failures in a cloak of heroic resistance. But what, then, of Cerdan? I think he's there but, for once, only in the idea of forgetting: he's among the '*chagrins*' she no longer needs, the 'loves' she's swept away. This is the imagined Piaf striving to rise above the narrative of personal tragedy and stride forward unencumbered. As delivered at the Olympia, the song is feminist in its rejection of subjugation and passivity, of a past where things were done to her, good or bad; a past she transcends by asserting agency. It's a musical palimpsest. There's the universal manifesto, the infinitely capacious cry of 'no!', and the hidden script of singer Édith Piaf conquering adversity and death not by acquiring another man in her life but by resurrecting her career and re-exerting her power over 'you', her audience. She's doing rather than being done to. Not victim but survivor.

## Track 8: 'La Belle Histoire d'amour' (the beautiful love story), Piaf-Dumont (pp.292–4)

To all appearances, this next track instantly contradicts the previous one. Just as much as 'Non, je ne regrette rien', the emotional hit comes from the total identification between the protagonist and the imagined Piaf, though here the Cerdan trope is much more in evidence. Piaf insisted on writing the lyric herself as soon as she heard Dumont's melody, which she was moved by. She completed it in a matter of hours. But she hadn't written the words alone, she insisted,[11] implying they were dictated by Cerdan just as she once believed she was receiving instructions from him at seances. It's certainly one of her better lyrics, in the sense that there's more emotional complexity and more to encourage us to read it as autobiography.

She examines her sexual adventurism after Cerdan with some lucidity, affirming the irresistible pull of desire in women as much as men. But its power isn't presented as unproblematic. Her avatar here is an experienced woman unburdened by sexual reticence, who uses men for pleasure and knows how to get what she wants. Yet she's also quick to 'excuse' that departure from contemporary gender norms. Whenever an attractive man shows interest, she always responds – blindly, recklessly. She tells us this succinctly in the lyric but it's articulated more forcefully in the full-throated, dramatic vocal and the two dissonant, brassy chordal stabs that announce each line of each verse. The chorus that follows then sets the record straight. She uses one-night stands to appease the loss of her one true love, her sexuality inseparable from the need to forget. Again, this is expressed lyrically but above all musically, through a much softer, lilting arrangement with a sentimental string accompaniment, as she evokes in flashback the beautiful story of love that now corrupts every new relationship. The traumatic tug-of-war between sex and love, verse and chorus, is tearing her asunder.

These tonal contrasts illuminate the whole song. The second verse details her complex reactions to loss: futile waiting and hoping, revolt and resignation, denial and prayer. But above all, anger at what she experiences as betrayal: why did he leave and why hasn't he come back? The third verse goes back to sex but with further insight. When she desires a man, she may well make the first move but, again, desire is instantly diverted into comparison. She perversely finds fault with him because what she really wants is a clone of the lost lover: it's his hand she longs to feel when the new lover touches her. The departed owns her, with all the agony and disempowerment this entails in her attempts to move on.

In the end there are two songs here, two states of mind and moral positions embodied in contrastive arrangements. Musically and vocally, the verses are characterized by bravado encompassing desire and anger. It's noticeable that in the brassiest moments, she even abandons the more oratorical apical /R/ for an especially throaty, phlegmy Parisian /R/. But in each chorus – melancholic, reflective, melodic – music and vocal speak of fidelity, duty, monogamous bliss. Taken together, these two modes equate female desire with sin, Catholic guilt. This is the tragic paradox within the Piaf avatar: she's a serially unfaithful monogamist. The two modes then fuse briefly in the last verse in so far as, even within those crashing decibels of desire, the lyric reinstates fidelity and hope: one day he will return, reach out and save her from moral turpitude. Yet this seeming resolution of the two modes is brittle, neurotic even. After she insists six times and with increasing frenzy that the departed will one day come back and carry her away, the arrangement explodes into six deafening, dissonant chords played by the horn section before the final climactic note of brass and percussion. In the live performance, all this sound and fury can only fully make sense through the audience's shared understanding that we're talking about Cerdan and that there's no chance whatsoever of his coming back. Indeed, the piercing discordance at the very end evokes the insanity of hope. However much one might want to distinguish between the singer and the narrative voice, as song theory tells us we should, lyrics and accompaniment in this song are a clear invitation to identify the Piaf-Cerdan myth as the inescapable subject matter. In yearning to justify her serial failure to settle into a new relationship, Piaf stages a psychologically absorbing drama of female sexual agency after loss. In this respect, it's a counterweight to the triumphalism of 'Non, je ne regrette rien', the two forming a tormented dialectic that leads directly into the last song on the album.

## Track 9: 'Les Blouses blanches' (roughly: the 'men in white coats'), Rivgauche-Monnot (pp.285–6)

This final track goes right out on a limb. As usual, Rivgauche's lyrics provide more narrative complexity than others' and Monnot's skilful melody was the only one by her to appear on the album. It was a daring or perhaps inspired choice to close the album, after the spirited uplift of 'Non, je ne regrette rien' and the tragic conflict of 'La Belle Histoire d'amour'. Certainly, 'Les Blouses blanches' is climactic and an obvious tour de force in performance. But it has an uncompromisingly dissonant arrangement which, coupled with Piaf's strident vocal, is painful to listen to. Little wonder, as it's about a woman locked in a psychiatric hospital against her will. According to legend, a spectator had to be carried out during one rendition. Piaf dropped the song several days later, fearing she herself might go mad singing it. Coquatrix had thought it unsingable but came to believe that she'd turned it into one of the greatest theatrical triumphs he'd ever witnessed.[12]

In a way, it follows logically from 'La Belle Histoire d'amour', as if the hint of neurosis in the former had eventually led the same woman to be sectioned. Similar too though more extreme are the disconcerting changes of tempo and mood. But, as with 'La Ville inconnue', the real power of the song lies in its cinematic nature, broadly reminiscent of a Hitchcockian psychological thriller or of the sinister film *Gaslight* (George Cukor, 1944) which depicts a woman persuaded by her husband that she's insane. The song begins with three instrumental layers: a repeated monotone played by the accordion, a regular percussive beat, and a recurrent four-beat piano arpeggio, the three layers together evoking the deranged ticking of a broken clock. Piaf's half-spoken voicing of the first lines has the same off-kilter bizarreness. This sonic evocation of perceived time is in fact a backcloth for the narrative, in which the woman trapped in the asylum for nearly three years loudly insists she isn't mad. It unfolds in the third person, so we don't see directly inside her head. But the accompaniment and Piaf's regressively child-like delivery indicate that she either is insane or has become so by being shut away unjustly. She violently protests that she's there by mistake but nobody believes or even listens to her, assuming she's just mad. This Kafkaesque quality is embodied in the ubiquitous white-coated staff, at whom she screams with growing frustration when they try to pacify her in soothing, infantilizing tones. But at one point the sight of the white coats seems to release a sublimated fragment of memory. A musical fade produces a change in tempo to a lyrical waltz with tender strings as, in a confused flashback, she recalls that she herself once wore white, which she first imagines was also *une blouse* (which means either a protective workcoat or a woman's blouse), before remembering that it was actually a pretty white dress with flowers. There was sunshine and a hand holding hers, its lovely fingers apparently 'singing'. Is this a recollection of a child with her parent, or of her wedding day, Miss Haversham-style? We have no idea, though we might guess at the latter as she says out of the blue: 'we'll love each other forever'. But at this point the mad clock starts up again.

In the second verse, the increasingly fragmented narrative reveals that another five years have passed. She wants to forget those years and threatens to 'steal' them back one day. But suddenly the disembodied hand reappears, described in an even more disconcertingly child-like voice. The unbearable screaming starts again as she continues to insist she isn't mad, until she reverts again to the child's voice, saying triumphantly that she knew her memory of the hand was real after all: this lovely hand that now, it would seem, was laughing. An association of ideas makes her move from the hand to the couple loving each other forever, briefly underscored by the gentle waltz time again. But that evocation, with its clichéd rhyming of 'amour' with 'toujours', is shockingly disrupted when she begins to chuckle, then laugh hysterically. In a sort of theatre of cruelty, Piaf delivers the laugh with increasing volume and a last ghastly cackle, as the band's accompaniment takes over, chiming relentlessly like the manic clock. Predictably, the performance brought the house down.

So what exactly is the place of this extraordinary song on the album? At one level, it's clearly intended to show off the reborn Piaf's remarkable capacity for vocal drama. Beyond that, I'd hazard two guesses. One is that the tale of madness completes the neurotic psychodrama of abandonment in 'La Belle Histoire d'amour', with the loss of Cerdan lurking in the background. Or perhaps that same beautiful love story is now being looked back on through the fragmenting prism of what we now call dementia. The other, related possibility is that the song concludes the album with an empathy-inducing reminder of Piaf's own recent experiences of confinement and institutionalization, at the mercy of men in white coats. Either way, her vocal performance of it was remarkable and a fitting end to an album showcasing a comeback.

*****

So, what can we conclude about the album as a whole? Although I don't know of any evidence to suggest an intentional thematic unity, I'd argue that on the threshold of the 1960s the raw material of the live recording has been edited into what would soon be called a concept album, where the constituent tracks are linked in a loose, not entirely linear narrative. The concept in this case is the imagined Piaf, still recognizable but updated and reconstructed. In particular, there are calculated allusions to the Cerdan story, as if she'd guessed that after being away for so long, she might need to remind audiences of the personal tragedy that has shaped her celebrity since 1949. But this is at the same time a re-imagined Piaf, who is now older, suffering, still in mourning yet defiantly challenging death. And embedded in this defiance are some less obvious dimensions. One inescapable observation is that her voice, as powerful and flexible as ever, still manages to both evoke and contrast with the tragic content of the songs. This had always been the case but on this album the contrast is intensified. With the help of Dumont's wider melodic range, the vocal crescendos coupled with the often explosive instrumental settings in songs like 'Les Blouses blanches', 'La Belle Histoire d'amour' and 'Non, je ne regrette rien' are expressions of triumph, agency, power. This raises the possibility that the delirious responses to her performance might have especially been due to the way her uncompromising vocals spoke directly to the audience of the inner strength and resilience that had allowed her to triumph over all the physical and romantic adversities alluded to directly or indirectly in her set. Most notably, the triumph of her restored voice is represented metaphorically in the narrative of resurrection in 'Non, je ne regrette rien'. Hence its special significance in the recital and in her story ever since.

This connects to a discreet element of regendering in the album. Certainly, some of her old realist tropes are revived, not least in the portrait on the sleeve: the pain of being a woman, whether hapless victim unable to reclaim the streets as in 'La Ville inconnue', or hopelessly dependent on men as in 'Mon Dieu'. But there are also green shoots emerging from this spent matter which, like her voice, embody the biographical message of triumph: over men, the body and death. There are also signs of a recasting of gender roles. This is conveyed with an entertainingly light touch in 'T'es l'homme qu'il me faut'; or in 'Mon vieux Lucien' where the weepy heartbreak is experienced by a man, while his anonymous pal is patently an insensitive buffoon. But the signs are clearest in 'Non, je ne regrette rien' where, rather than the forlorn lamentations of a broken-hearted girl, we see a mature, self-possessed woman refusing to be held back by her past and determined to shape her future. There are traces of this in 'La Belle Histoire' too, where one of the two 'voices' is that of a modern woman enjoying sexual agency. But in this case the overall meaning is ambiguous since agency is presented as poor compensation for a lost man. This ambiguity is in fact an unresolved leitmotiv throughout the album, but especially on side 2. There's in fact a detectable arc in the four tracks that make up the second side, if we take the women in them as a single avatar of the imagined Piaf. The edgy, abandoned woman of 'La Ville inconnue', chained to her past, finally frees herself in 'Non, je ne regrette rien', which forms the summit of the arc. But in the next track, 'La Belle Histoire d'amour', she's already coming down the other side. Her confidence in her self-liberation is weakening, as she's sucked back into a corrosive obsession with the past that leads to psychological disturbance and ultimately, in 'Les Blouses blanches', sequestration. In an ironic reversal of the Christ motif that has underpinned the whole comeback discourse, side 2's composite female protagonist moves from resurrection to crucifixion.

We probably can't call this a feminist album, because seemingly Piaf wasn't ready to jettison the persona that had underpinned her whole career, a persona firmly restated in that portrait on the sleeve. But there's enough to suggest a transition in her choice of material – both lyrical and of course compositional given Dumont's refreshingly different melodies – to an assertiveness more in line with her off-stage personality. This ties in with the presence of a mature, lucid awareness of the complex nature of emotions. Which in turn leads to an intriguing characteristic of the album itself: an emerging meta dimension, a self-referential awareness of the nature and power of popular song and even in some tracks a watermark of other songs selected for it. Thanks to the recording of the live concert, reshaped into an LP which stands on its own merits, the last major motif in the imagining of the living Piaf is essentially survival, resilience and artistic self-knowledge. On the threshold of the 1960s, that great era of moral and cultural and sexual change, the narrative of her physical resurrection is matched by an embryonic re-imagining of her musically and thematically. At just forty-five years old at the end of 1960, who knows where that re-imagining might have taken her? The irony of course was that she didn't live long enough for anyone to find out. Nevertheless, the concert and the album did transform what she would go on to mean after her death, as we'll see next.

# 5   Authenticity, Art, Memory, Stardom

Over the last six decades, the Olympia engagement has been seminal in the making of the Piaf myth. In the light of her death and regardless of chronology, it can so easily be read as her swan song, the final full-stop in a narrative. And, as the numbers who witnessed the first night have dwindled, it's the LP that has maintained its position in the cultural imagination, helping shape her national and global meanings. I want to try to identify the most enduring themes embedded in the imagining of Piaf after the concert, some of them placed there by her own last efforts to build a legacy, others materializing as a result of her early death.

One of the most obvious themes is invincibility in suffering. Her return after months of life-threatening illness did most of the spade work for her, though she did a lot of the labouring herself. Hugues Vassal recalls that after every illness she would ask him to take a picture: 'She wanted to show she was strong, courageous, that she was going to make a comeback once again.'[1] Her selection of tracks and cover art for the album also drove the point home. In this respect, *Récital 1961* can be seen as documenting a comeback *about* a comeback. But behind this self-referentiality, I think there's an ambition to communicate a related message about 'authenticity', a capacious term that would preoccupy popular music in the 1960s and after.

Allan Moore sees one of its meanings as being 'authenticity of expression' or 'first-person authenticity'. This 'arises when an originator (composer, performer) succeeds in conveying the impression that his/her utterance is one of integrity, that it represents an attempt to communicate in an unmediated form with an audience'. The audience is in fact the key here, for 'authenticity is ascribed to, rather than inscribed in, a performance'.[2] Piaf specialist Joëlle-Andrée Deniot argues that by the time her career took off in the 1930s, French audiences were already starting to want singers to be not just a voice but a person, exposing their own emotions and frailties so that the spectator could identify with them. This began with the realist singer Fréhel but developed considerably with Piaf.[3] From the start, the young Édith's outward appearance was enough to suggest that her realist songs were directly about her. But she also did a great deal to favour that impression, building a repertoire that matched her experience but recounting her experience to match the repertoire. The Olympia comeback took this authenticity-building to a new level. Talking to Michèle Manceaux after the first night about her recent misfortunes, she declared they weren't really misfortunes at all: 'thanks to this experience, I can understand what I sing, I can be what I am'.[4] The show was duly praised in the same terms. For Manceaux, 'Édith Piaf displays her bleeding heart, she screams it'.[5] For Sarraute, her banal songs of love and hope 'belong to her. Just as much as the astonishing way she stages them, what matters to us is their sincerity, obvious and admitted to.'[6] This sincerity was even thought to be catalytic, inspiring each member of the audience, especially women, to recognize their own experience in hers. It was a managed moment of one-to-one empathy. A young Roland Barthes, scribbling notes for a lecture about popular music in 1948, had already recognized this distinctive quality in Piaf, albeit with the usual critical (male) appraisal of her body. The realist singer

Damia, he maintains, offers only a commercial caricature of the people, 'realism for the rich'. Piaf, on the other hand, 'a small, not very young, not very attractive woman, in a cheap-looking little black dress' and with 'a slightly rasping voice, not in the least sugary, slightly harsh and bitter', represents the reality of those working-class women who take the metro four times a day and spend their one day off doing chores. Like them, Piaf 'fully accepts her poverty' and in so doing 'expresses the tragic sadness of the common people in the grip of a fate that is beyond them'.[7] Of course, not many working-class women could have afforded a ticket to the show; but they might just have run to buying the record.

Barthes's comments point to a second type of authenticity that Piaf projected that night. As Moore argues, the term may also refer to 'the importance of retaining a point of origin', truth to one's cultural roots and experience, as with the original blues singers of the deep south.[8] This too can be applied to Piaf at the Olympia. Even though she'd become a global celebrity by the 1950s, for her home audiences there was always something reassuringly local about her. Paris had long been tattooed on the image of this one-time street waif born in Belleville and later discovered singing in a ripe Parisian accent on a corner in the upmarket Étoile area. It had been written into the songs too, either explicitly in references to districts like Montparnasse, Clignancourt or Pigalle or as their implied setting. In her early numbers, the urban environment is working-class, run-down, marginalized and threatening. From around 1945, she tried to distance herself from such grubby associations, aspiring to more universal appeal. But to the end of her days and beyond, she was synonymous in the collective imagination, at home and abroad, with the social periphery of her native city. This Paris challenges the standard tourist images: it's neither the capital of high fashion, art and literature, nor the cosmopolitan locus of jazz and avant-garde cabarets. And yet it isn't the Paris of 1960 either. It's a populist Paris in the sense that it spurns elites, but in doing so it looks back to a semi-fictional, pre-war city, and even in some ways the Paris of the late 1800s, where today's suburbs were still known as *faubourgs* and the old fortified walls (*les fortifs*) had yet to be swept away by the brutalist ring road. It evokes louche but romanticized locations where sex workers lean seductively on lampposts and gangs of youths known as *apaches* in butcher-boy caps roam the streets with a characteristic rolling gait. So, her songs sidestep one myth of Paris but substitute another, already outdated by 1960 when the capital was developing economically, demographically and architecturally at a pace. Most noticeably, there's no hint in her Paris of its expanding ethnic mix; no sign that her native Belleville had long seen successive waves of inward migration. And certainly no sign of North Africans or her own Moroccan heritage. But this is precisely the point. Paradoxically, temporal and ethnic dislocation is integral to her particular version of 'local' authenticity and to the complicity it creates with her Parisian audiences. The imagined Piaf requires what Benedict Anderson calls an imagined community – imagined because it's a cultural construct rather than a social reality.[9] The Olympia recital was the celebration of an assumed bond connecting her to the people's Paris, irrespective of how much the audience had actually paid to get in. And that bond depended on her representing a lost, white Paris of memory and myth.

When he coined the term 'imagined communities', Anderson was mainly thinking about nations and nationalism. And in the highly centralized France of 1960, Paris was virtually a metonym for the entire French polity. By the same token, a Piaf concert in the capital might be represented as a national conversation, as if she were singing for a whole people with whom she shared not just a language but a worldview. Or, as biographer Carolyn Burke writes, 'as if Piaf's voice evoked a national consensus'.[10] Better still, with her apparent triumph over her martyred body and her new songs about love and defiance, the Olympia concert seemed to symbolize the immutability of a 'French character' and its irrepressible capacity for resistance. Reports of her being described abroad, especially in the States, as archetypally French only fed back into this sense of territorial identity. One Parisian journalist, after she'd been hospitalized in New York City with an ulcer in 1959, observed: 'When they listen to Édith Piaf, what the Americans in the Waldorf Astoria or Carnegie Hall are hearing is France singing. An ulcer couldn't silence a voice like that.'[11] Thirty-six years later, another, writing when the film *La Vie en rose* was released in 2007, explained her popularity in the United States: 'she is Paris, she is France, cheerful, mocking, miserable, eternal France'.[12] Her authenticity, then, is at once local and national.

Responses to the recital also show that her work by then was being taken seriously as a popular art, elevating the status of French music hall in a country still fixated on its historic literary and artistic achievements. A year before the comeback, de Gaulle's transformation of French governance had included the setting up of France's first fully fledged department for the arts, the Ministry of Cultural Affairs, under the award-winning novelist and art theorist André Malraux. The new minister devised a state conception of 'culture' that mirrored his own reflexions on the purpose of high art and that repudiated mass culture, supposedly composed of 'imbecilic' products for passive consumption, whereas true art stretched the human soul. His problem was that the cultural activities of the majority population didn't include a lot of soul-stretching, at least not of the kind he had in mind. Television was beginning to reach more French homes by 1960, albeit state-run. The commercial radio stations Europe no. 1 and RTL were pumping out American-style pop music and jazz, which were steadily altering French listening practices. But at that very moment, descriptions of Piaf's Olympia performances were hinting that chanson, rooted in a specifically French tradition, might just be subverting Malraux's high/low binary: not frivolous or garbled or amplified or foreign, but noble and uplifting yet without requiring any particular level of educational attainment. What the Olympia show demonstrated, just when teenage singers like Hallyday were impersonating American styles and said to be corrupting the tastes of French youth, was the persistent appeal of a more traditional, 'authentically French' popular song form, a national middlebrow that deserved a specific stamp of legitimation as 'la chanson *française*'.

Musicologist Catherine Rudent maintains that *la chanson française* can't meaningfully be called a genre because it's so diverse sonically and stylistically. Its cultural significance has therefore to be more symbolic than musical.[13] She is surely right. It's a discursive shorthand that carries with it a distinction between lightweight commercial 'pop' – *variétés* as it's long been known in French, mostly with disparaging connotations – and lyrically more ambitious works in French expressing personal emotion or reflection.[14] In this respect, there's a parallel with the contemporaneous rise of the French cinematic auteur. In the 1950s, the idea of the director as author, centralizing all aspects of filmmaking and expressing a personal or autobiographical vision, had been theorized, particularly by François Truffaut in his film criticism. By the time of Piaf's comeback, it had generated the French New Wave, represented by directors like Jean-Luc Godard, Claude Chabrol and Truffaut himself. Although no equivalent theory had been applied to chanson, the emergence at much the same time of the so-called 'text-song' (*chanson à texte*) produced by independently minded 'poetic' singer-songwriters was pushing in a similar direction. Jacques Brel, Georges Brassens and Léo Ferré were unintentionally forming into a triumvirate of multi-talented 'author-composer-singers' – as they are revealingly known in French – personifying a quasi-literary national idiom indebted to Charles Trenet. Piaf herself, although she wrote many songs, has never been admitted to this exclusive, hyphenated, predominantly male club, but she is undoubtedly their other 1930s ancestor, alongside Trenet. Certainly, her practice of controlling every aspect of her output and image is a form of auteurism. And her meticulous staging of her comeback – gesture, physical appearance, lighting, arrangements, and of course the choice of song and the production of the album – was the climax of that practice, contributing greatly to the artistic prestige she enjoys today.

In this context, the word 'recital' becomes significant. This was the first of her four Olympia LPs to use it, the previous ones all using '*tour de chant*' instead, redolent of the old music halls. As we saw, the practice of having diverse types of act to entertain the audience, of which the singer was only one, had faded in the 1920s and 1930s as cinema, radio, records and the microphone allowed a more intimate relationship between singer and public.[15] By 1960, Aznavour, Trenet and Montand, preceded by Chevalier with his one-man shows in France and the States, were adopting the recital formula, where they were the only act on the bill, as is common today. This was more than just a functional shift. Hirschi calls it the 'sacralization of a cult in which only the singing star counts, in ever more gigantic places of worship',[16] a development leading eventually to the spectacular stadium events of recent times. Piaf's 1960 show was different to the extent that she still included other types of act in the first half while she occupied the second. But the experience of sacralization was the same, embedded in fact in the very word 'recital', which she re-used for her last Olympia album in 1962. With its classical connotations, the idea of giving a recital elevates the singer from music-hall act to artist.

Around this time, she in fact speaks of her work in terms that suggest artistic inspiration, aspiration and dedication. 'I always go right on to the end', she told Pierre Desgraupes; 'I wasn't afraid of dying because if I couldn't sing I didn't want to live'. 'When I sing, I feel as though I don't belong to myself anymore, I'm no longer there, [I go into] a kind of trance.'[17] With her eye firmly on her posterity, she's falling back here on an essentially Romantic art discourse in order to imply that the chanson performer is much more than a light entertainer. Others do the same when speaking about her. 'This Piaf who is as important as, if not more than la Callas', the classical choreographer Roland Petit would call her.[18] The Olympia concert played a vital part in her ennoblement as a benchmark of artistic authenticity in chanson. Just a year later, when the more lightweight singer Dalida first appeared there after recently converting to pop, she was sent an anonymous funeral wreath bearing the cruel message, 'In memory of the late lamented chanson, long live Édith Piaf'.[19]

So Piaf's return to the stage was crucial to her posterity in a number of ways. It strengthened perceptions of her authenticity, local, national and musical; it confirmed her as an icon of both the people's Paris and a more comprehensive sense of national identity; and it helped establish *la chanson française* as an auteurist medium. These themes built into the imagining of Piaf at the end of her life point to another, which has only become discernible since her death. In 2007, when the biopic came out, a journalist speculated why she still touches the French today: 'To understand this mystery, we have no doubt to look beyond the singing and call to mind her destiny, that French story that has turned her into a *lieu de mémoire*.'[20] This is a reference to an influential work by a team of French historians under Pierre Nora, translated as *Realms of Memory*, though 'memory site' is also used. With this term, Nora aims 'to define France as a reality that is entirely symbolic'.[21] In a postmodern, global world, the old sacred rituals of collective memory that once helped bind communities have vanished. Yet a deep yearning for such rituals persists. *Lieux de mémoire*, then, 'are fundamentally vestiges, the ultimate embodiments of a commemorative consciousness that survives in a history which, having renounced memory, cries out for it'.[22] Hence the contemporary tendency to memorialize everything, to retrieve the past in reconstructed form: national celebrations, anniversaries, museums, genealogy and so on. And essential to this tendency are a number of fondly remembered, totemic personalities. Anniversaries of Piaf's birth and death continue to be marked; the songs are regularly repackaged in boxsets; and biographies, memoirs and of course books like the present one are still handing down her story as if it were a folk memory. In an age when culture is mostly consumed privately, retelling the Piaf saga can be seen as a ritual for restoring a collective narrative.

The Olympia comeback was in my estimate the trigger for this memorialization of her. Even at the time, there was a ceremonial, ritual quality to it. It was said that the audience came in order to be part of something historic, even if it was only to see her die. But as usual Piaf was way ahead of them. Nora claims that all memory sites contain 'representations of themselves'. In her case, after those long months of absence and

Authenticity, Art, Memory, Stardom

the prospect of dying, she seems fully aware of the symbolic potential of her return and decides to exploit and take control of it while she still can. Everything about the way she stages it suggests she is knowingly directing a set-piece performance of her imagined life, an artful cameo of what she wants the audience to remember. It's as if she's saying: 'You're all familiar with my story. Let me frame it for you one last time so that you get it right when it's turned into a collective memory.' As if she's already claiming a seat for herself in the national pantheon.

A related theme in representations of her after the comeback does indeed concern her position in musical history, both French and global. As we've seen, by the mid-1950s she had achieved international standing, but an unintended consequence was that her star had begun to wane a little at home. By spending a total of twenty-five months touring the Americas, she was neglecting her French fans, except for a few short months in 1956 when she did a sell-out twelve weeks at the Olympia. On her second homecoming in August 1957, she tried to re-establish her position by frantic activity, including the publication in 1958 of her first autobiography, *The Wheel of Fortune*.[23] Between February and April that year, she was back at the Olympia for another record-breaking stint. More touring followed, leading eventually to the suicide tour of 1959 and the year-long absence from the stage. Another nascent problem at home was that she was coming to look just a little dated, as the French scene had started to move on during her absences. She was now an establishment figure while younger women were appearing with fashionable new styles, like Gloria Lasso and Dalida, both working in sexy exoticism complete with foreign origins and accents. By 1957, Dalida was outranking Édith in terms of sales and popularity.[24] Then there was the cooler denizen of the Left Bank, Juliette Gréco, the 'muse' of the existentialists. Although her repertoire was more bohemian and her style quite different, Gréco was hailed as the new Piaf and Édith saw her as a threat, particularly when Gréco occasionally strayed into her territory. There was also the young singer Barbara who was being noticed in Left-Bank cabaret. On the male side, the emerging singer-songwriters had intellectual credentials while Édith's protégés, most notably Montand and Aznavour, were making it on their own as crooners combining chanson with a jazzy, more American sound. And finally, as we've seen, there was American rock'n'roll.

So, one clear meaning her comeback conveyed, as it was intended to, was that she wasn't a has-been. After all, this was the international Piaf who'd wowed Carnegie Hall twice. In French coverage of the opening Olympia shows, there was a marked emphasis on her world standing, evidenced in the presence of stars of stage and screen. There was even an apocryphal story that Presidents Kennedy and Khrushchev had sent her good luck telegrams for the start of her show. True or not, it shows an awareness and a deliberate foregrounding of her importance as a global star. Much attention was also given to her being the only singer big enough to save Coquatrix's Olympia. Here she now was, international celebrity, back from the dead, battle-hardened elder stateswoman of chanson armed with new lyrics, new tunes and a new assertiveness, adored anew every night by devoted audiences. And 'Non, je ne regrette rien' perfectly drew attention to this resurrection: she was embracing the new decade by 'setting fire' to the past.

So, I believe there were concerted attempts, by herself and others, to position her at the Olympia not as a nostalgic relic unable to adapt to a new age but as a redeeming angel summoned back to reconcile the two cultures. Johnny Hallyday, decadent herald of teenage philistinism, was reported to adore her[25] and would later perform 'Hymne à l'amour' and 'Non, je ne regrette rien'. Dumont, remembering her comeback nearly half a century later, describes her as the 'lynch-pin' between the *chanson réaliste* and a new generation: 'the end of the old era and the start of the new'.[26] I think she returned to the Olympia determined to modernize. Her forerunners had established the realist song as a genre characterized by nostalgia and a derivative version of nineteenth-century naturalism. Starting her career in the mid-1930s, Piaf borrowed its conventions but systematically updated them as the years went by, taking it into the age of records and other mass media and giving it different, late-twentieth-century resonances. One purpose of her adoption of Dumont was to stretch herself by altering her repertoire and sound. She'd returned from the United States aware of the threat from rock'n'roll, having seen Elvis on the Ed Sullivan show. And there are echoes of it in her late work, for example Dumont's 'Le Billard électrique' (The pinball machine, 1961), with its racy American sound and a nod to teen culture. In 1963, she would write the words for a song for Sarapo called 'La Bande en noir' (The gang in black) about violence between adolescent bikers, which even referenced *La Fureur de vivre*, the French title of James Dean's *Rebel without a Cause*.

Nevertheless, the new Piaf couldn't afford not to be the old one. Her failed love affairs after Cerdan, her health and physical appearance, the five car accidents, had all constructed a fruitful public narrative in which a doom presided over her, which that portrait on the album sleeve invokes. The comeback also played on it but discreetly updated and redirected it. As we saw, the narrative of fate came to be counterbalanced by a discourse of triumph over it. A dialectic between predestined destruction and some form of heroic reassertion of self had been the stuff of tragedy since the classical age, but she came to incarnate it in a pop-cultural iteration. Re-routing the realist song, she turned the melodramatic victim of the cover portrait into the tragic diva, still vigorous today in global popular culture from Billie Holiday and Judy Garland to Whitney Houston and Amy Winehouse. Hence the international tendency since her death to recreate her story in theatre, films, documentaries, songs and tribute acts or albums. Hence, too, the worldwide afterlife of 'Non, je ne regrette rien' founded on the figure of the female survivor which would later become so familiar in popular song: Gloria Gaynor's 'I Will Survive', Donna Summer and Barbra Streisand's 'Enough Is Enough', and any number of US country songs by women. She didn't invent the transnational tragic diva but she was proactive in shaping and gallicizing it. And it's an essential part of what has made her a global star.

Stardom is another especially important theme in the imagined Piaf. The 1950s had cemented her status as what we mean today by a 'celebrity': someone whose career relies on the public's assumed thirst for role-models to mythify and see demythified. From the death of Cerdan in 1949 through the 1950s, Piaf's personal life was pored over by the media: travels, love affairs, wealth and health. The reporting of the Olympia recital was the pinnacle of this attention, with its narratives of miraculous resurrection and glitzy admiration from showbiz royalty, deploying the codes familiar today in soaps: pathos, courageous 'battles' with illness, irrepressible rags-to-riches ordinariness and so on. But celebrity isn't stardom, particularly not today when 'celeb' is applied to virtually anyone on television, however fleetingly and whatever their talent. In the anglophone world, star theory has relied particularly on Richard Dyer's pioneering work on the ideological subtexts of Hollywood stars.[27] Less known internationally but equally important is the French social theorist Edgar Morin.[28] He recognizes that by the mid-twentieth century the star manufactured by the Hollywood studio system had come to fill a deep cultural need. What fans of classic Hollywood movies gained from them was the opportunity to identify with their favourite star as if she or he were one of them, but also simultaneously to project their own drab, contingent existence onto those figures and see it magnified and essentialized on screen.

Morin's analysis of this 'identification-projection' in movie stardom can also be applied to music. What characterized the commercial strategies of the great international record companies as vinyl became established was multimedia synergy.[29] In France, this began in the 1950s when key industry figures like Canetti and Coquatrix started combining in their own professional activities the resources of records, live performance and radio; and it progressed considerably with television. This synergy led to some performers acquiring a symbolic significance greater than that of mere celebrities and Piaf was an early example. In the 1950s, she added TV appearances to her portfolio of live shows, records, radio and press, as with her interviews on *Cinq colonnes à la une*. The star persona that this engendered helps make sense of the extraordinary adulation at her Olympia recital. Stardom is more than the sum of its parts. Identification-projection requires the star to be what Morin calls a semi-divinity, at once human and god-like, accessible and remote. By the end of her life, she had achieved exactly that, combining the common touch with the ineffability of the sacred. On one occasion, going out to buy aspirin, she was recognized. People knelt, kissed her hand or offered up their infant to be touched.[30] And at the recital itself, the warm response to her acknowledging the mistake with 'Mon vieux Lucien' was of the same order. She was divinely fallible.

# Conclusions: The Two Piafs

The representations of Piaf I've just outlined have made her one of the great icons of global culture. Certainly, other French singers have achieved international fame: Françoise Hardy, Josephine Baker (born American but naturalized French), Serge Gainsbourg, Maurice Chevalier, Charles Aznavour. But none with quite the same symbolic force. More than any of her other shows, that Olympia first night, the album that has immortalized it and the song from it whose title has become a universal alibi for impenitence, have influenced the way she's remembered, turning her into a memory site for France and the world. But if she's still out there like a long-lost satellite, transmitting meanings at us from beyond the grave, I think we need to be clearer about precisely which Piaf is transmitting them.

Throughout this book, I've referred to an imagined Piaf, but I think there are actually two of them circulating today. The years pass and their passing turns dead celebrities, like all of us, into cliché. Slipping ever further from its flesh-and-blood moorings over the last sixty years, the dominant imagined Piaf has become a transnational metaphor open to infinite uses. Her name instantly calls to mind a heart-wrenching voice, a tragic life, soap-opera feistiness and a mythical Paris. Its perennial appeal was demonstrated again in 2021 by yet another production of Pam Gems's 1978 play *Piaf*, this time in Leeds and Nottingham. Excellent though the play is, it actually paints a rather approximate picture of the singer's life and character, read through an English lens and stylized for dramatic purposes. Even the more detailed biopic *La Vie en rose* has a similar tendency to recycle the familiar tropes: neglect in childhood, rags to riches, heartbreak and so on. Some of these tropes are accurate, of course, though most were embellished or even generated by Piaf herself. Nevertheless, they've been condensed with the passage of time into a handful of snapshots, stock images. Singers performing tribute shows, like Martha Wainwright in 2009 or Patricia Kaas in 2012, fall back on those images for their own artistic purposes, which then shape future perceptions, placing in the public domain a kind of cartoon Piaf. This was brought home to me after a performance of Gems's play that my family and I attended, when one departing audience member was overheard summarizing what they'd just learnt about her: 'so basically Piaf was about whores, death, and dead whores.'[1] Having admittedly made her debut exploiting narratives of this kind, she did work hard to break free of them, while also benefiting from them. But this is where *Récital 1961* provides a useful corrective, revealing a second, differently imagined Piaf.

'Records made her a star.'[2] This assessment in an exhibition marking the centenary of her birth may sound surprising, but it's true. She was a product of the recording industry from the outset, from 'L'Étranger' (The stranger) recorded in 1935 to 'L'Homme de Berlin' (The man from Berlin), her last recording, made six months before she died. Yet in the public imagination, she's the archetypally live performer, starting on the Paris streets and ending up at the Olympia. The English word 'live' has long been rendered in French as 'en direct',[3] which deceptively implies unmediated communication between singer and public. But since 1963, the 'live' Édith Piaf has only been accessible in mediated form: on record, in films and documentaries, in tribute shows and clips on YouTube, in adverts, ring tones and karaoke downloads. So the live album is the only way for us to access her today in anything like her flesh-and-blood reality. And no other live record does more to reveal the second imagined Piaf than *Récital 1961*, not only because of the quality of the performance but because it has made it possible for new generations to at least partially experience this uniquely important event and interpret it in their own ways. It has made that performance legendary but it also allows us, if we look closely enough, to see her more clearly. Although on that album she's still using a few of the realist tropes she began with, she's working now with a much wider palette of styles and emotions. Sixty years on, the disc gives the attentive listener a more rounded experience of what she meant.

I argued earlier that Piaf required her lyricists to write from within her biography but that she also adapted that biography to match her lyrics. She did this increasingly as her fame grew, particularly after Cerdan. This two-way self-narration seems to me to come to a head with the Olympia comeback, which, as I've tried to show, turns the record into a proto-concept album, where the concept is the post-Cerdan, post-illness, disillusioned but still hopeful singer at the top of her game. Within this latest and last projection lie a self-assertion and a mature realism about romance, men and women, and sex that half-point towards the feminism of the 1960s and 1970s, although there's possibly too much remaining of the former Piaf to go much further than that. Even so, it's revealing that for some time now she's been cited as a model, influence or symbol for younger anglophone women – Anna Calvi, Martha Wainwright, Lady Gaga and others. And emerging French chanteuses have long identified with her or been identified as new Piafs, from Mireille Mathieu in the 1960s to the young reality-show star Camélia Jordana and France's near-winner of Eurovision in 2021, Barbara Pravi. In 2020, a book accompanying a film, both entitled *Haut les filles*,[4] published interviews with ten women in French rock from Françoise Hardy and Brigitte Fontaine through Charlotte Gainsbourg to Camélia Jordana. The singers themselves don't have all that much to say about Piaf though several reference her; but the publicity for the film does, suggesting rather surprisingly that the 'passion' characterizing female rock in France might well have begun with Piaf's 'Hymne à l'amour':

> Although history dates the birth of rock'n'roll back to Elvis's 'Heartbreak Hotel' in 1954, for us this universal gospel song by Piaf, the Kabyle diva from Belleville, is the birth certificate of rock'n'roll passion. Everything that the music of the century would go on to be is there: midway between lament and blues, it's a bolt of lightning, a cry in the night.[5]

Even more significantly in the context of #MeToo, broad associations between Piaf and new women's movements are becoming more frequent. To mark the fortieth anniversary of the International Day of Women's Rights in March 2017, France's National Audiovisual Institute (INA) produced a short video entitled 'Thank you Édith Piaf': 'You offered your heart, you touched our souls, you opened the way. Thank you Édith'.[6] And the point is illustrated with clips from the December 1960 *Cinq colonnes* interview and, inevitably, her performance there of 'Non, je ne regrette rien'. In her book on women in popular music, Lucy O'Brien notes how unusual it was in Piaf's time for a woman in the music business to be in control of her career and she goes on to describe Piaf as 'a symbol of a mordant delicate sensuality in an era when the mainstream was gorging itself on the blonde-bombshell dynamic of pin-up stars like Betty Grable'.[7] The travel website Culture Trip even lists Piaf among the ten women who have changed French history, alongside Joan of Arc, the eighteenth-century feminist and abolitionist Olympe de Gouges, Marie Curie and Simone de Beauvoir.[8]

What, then, is most striking in *Récital 1961* today, what in fact becomes visible at its very heart, is a mature, clear-eyed, self-possessed awareness. One focus of that awareness, most evident in 'La Ville inconnue', is the vulnerability of women in a society made by men. But another is a woman's freedom to rise above that vulnerability and reclaim her life. This freedom is at its most vocal in 'Non, je ne regrette rien', but it's also there less emphatically in 'T'es l'homme qu'il me faut', 'Les Mots d'amour', and even, in extremis, in the lonely refusal of madness in 'Les Blouses blanches'.

A third focus of awareness, perhaps the most subtle given Piaf's artistic medium, concerns popular music itself. In 'Les Mots d'amour' and 'Les Flonflons du bal', music shapes emotions, inflaming them, exaggerating them, even producing them. However, this particular form of awareness is most apparent not in individual songs but in the self-presentation of that spectral figure standing uncertainly but unbowed on the Olympia stage in December 1960. Her meticulous staging of her body, the inflexions of her voice, the economy of her interactions with the audience, the musical settings she chooses for each song and the tracks she selects for the album, all indicate an artist fully aware of the potency of popular song and of her resulting power over her public – a power which, after a prolonged period of inactivity, incapacity and desolation, she's resolved to reclaim. This above all is the Édith Piaf that *Récital 1961* urges us, its listeners, to imagine in the twenty-first century.

END

# Notes

## Chapter 1

**1**    FSX 133 mono. The album's title doesn't indicate the date of the actual live recording but the year most of her Olympia engagement took place. A misleadingly titled *Olympia 61 vol.2* (Columbia/EMI SCTX 340.466) is in fact a 1963 re-release after her death, containing exactly the same tracks but with a new sleeve design. There was a further vinyl re-release in 1983, the twentieth anniversary of her death, as the fourth in a six-volume collection on Pathé-Marconi / EMI (115 304–1). The revised title printed on the back cover was *Olympia 61 Non, je ne regrette rien.* See http://www.encyclopedisque.fr/recherche.html to search her discography.

**2**    *Billboard Music Week*, 16 January 1961, 14. (Later just *Billboard*). Official music charts didn't exist in France in 1961, so this placement must be the estimate of the magazine's Paris correspondent Eddie Adamis, tasked with drawing up something like a French hit parade, though how he did so isn't known. See Muz Hit! 'The French Charts Are Celebrating Their 35th Anniversary. Or Is It Their 58th?'. Available online: https://muzhit.com/?p=384 (accessed 1 February 2022).

**3**    Jean Noli, *Piaf secrète* (Paris: L'Archipel, 1973), 45.

**4**    Fabrice Ferment, correspondence with the author, 25 November–13 December 2021. Ferment wrote *40 ans de tubes 1960–2000: les meilleures ventes de 45 tours & CD Singles* (Paris: Larivière, 2001) and is in charge of the site http://www.top-france.fr.

**5**  Respectively FS 1049 (released 1955), FS 1065 (released 1956) and FS 1075 (released 1958).

**6**  David Looseley, *Édith Piaf: A Cultural History* (Liverpool: Liverpool University Press, 2015).

**7**  Ibid., 151.

**8**  See, for example, Lucy O'Brien, *She Bop: The Definitive History of Women in Popular Music*, rev. edn (London: Jawbone, 2020), who describes Piaf as 'one of [cabaret's] greatest exponents'. 47.

**9**  Looseley, *Édith Piaf*, 42.

**10**  Hugues Vassal, *Dans l'intimité des stars, le spectacle*' (Paris: L'Archipel, 2019), 37. Vassal can also be heard telling this story in a video, available online: https://www.hugues-vassal.com/show-biz (accessed 4 February 2022).

**11**  Apparently, neither Aznavour nor Dumont became her lovers.

**12**  Marc Robine, *Il était une fois la chanson française* (Paris: Fayard/Livre de Poche, 2004), 75–81.

**13**  Quoted in David Bret, *Édith Piaf the Untold Story: Find Me a New Way to Die* (London: Oberon Books, 2015), 124.

**14**  Charles Dumont, *Non, je ne regrette toujours rien* (Paris: Calmann-Lévy, 2012), 102.

**15**  Quoted in Bernard Marchois, *Piaf: emportée par la foule* (Paris: Éditions du Collectionneur; Vade Retro, 1993), 128.

**16**  Gilles Verlant (ed.), *Olympia Bruno Coquatrix: 50 ans de music-hall* (Paris: Éditions Hors Collection, 2003), 43.

**17**  Quoted in Bret, *Édith Piaf*, 121.

**18**  *Cinq colonnes à la une* [TV programme]. Interview with Piaf, RTF, 2 December 1960. Available at www.ina.fr/video/I00000109/edith-piaf-avant-sanouvelle-tournee-video.html (accessed 2 February 2022).

**19**  From the various contemporary accounts and often imprecise biographies and personal recollections, it's not always certain which celebrities attended the first night and which the gala premiere on 2 January. But these ones seem most likely to have been at the first night.

**20**  Doudou Morizot, correspondence with the author, undated (February 2022); and Morizot, *Je les ai tous vus débuter* (Paris: L'Archipel, 2021), 50–2.

**21**  Michèle Manceaux, 'Piaf ressuscitée', *L'Express*, 4 January 1961.

**22**  Quoted in Bret, *Édith Piaf*, 121.

**23**  Morizot, correspondence. Various accounts time the applause differently but all agree that it lasted a remarkably long time.

**24**  Noli, *Piaf secrète*, 51.

**25**  Morizot, correspondence; Dumont, *Non*, 115.

**26**  Andrée Deniot, *Édith Piaf la voix, le geste, l'icône: esquisse anthropologique* (Paris: Lelivredart, 2012), 254.

**27**  Quoted in Robert Belleret, *Piaf: un mythe français* (Paris: Fayard, 2013), 706–7.

**28**  Édith Piaf, *My Life*, trans. M. Crosland (London: Penguin, 1992).

**29**  Morizot, *Je les ai tous vus débuter*, 52–3 and quoted in Emmanuel Bonini, *Piaf: la vérité* (Paris: Pygmalion, 2008), 501.

# Chapter 2

**1**  Dumont, *Non*, 115 and 116, respectively.

**2**  *Discorama* [TV programme]. Interview with Piaf by Paul Giannoli, 20 January 1961. Not broadcast. Available at https://

www.ina.fr/ina-eclaire-actu/video/cpf03007301/edith-piaf (accessed 28 January 2022).

3 Manceaux, 'Piaf ressuscitée'.

4 Quoted in Bonini, *Piaf*, 475.

5 Quoted in Verlant (ed.), *Olympia*, 43 and various other accounts.

6 Quoted in Bernard Marchois, *La Vraie Piaf: témoignages et portraits inédits* (Paris: Éditions Didier Carpentier, 2013), 149.

7 Quoted in ibid.

8 Quoted in Belleret, *Piaf*, 703–4.

9 Hugues Vassal, *Dans les pas de … Édith Piaf* (Paris: Éditions Les Trois Orangers, 2002), 16–17.

10 Ibid., 18.

11 Quoted in Looseley, *Édith Piaf*, 71.

12 Pierre Leuzinger, 'Résurrection de Piaf', *Tribune de Genève*, 7 January 1961.

13 Manceaux, 'Piaf ressuscitée'.

14 Ibid.

15 Leuzinger, 'Résurrection de Piaf'.

16 Quoted in Marchois, *Piaf*, 128.

17 Claude Sarraute, 'Édith Piaf à l'Olympia', *Le Monde*, 31 December 1960.

18 Jean-Noël Gurgand, 'Édith Piaf: la boucle est bouclée', *France Observateur*, 5 January 1961.

19 Deniot, *Édith Piaf*, 133 and *passim*.

20 For more detailed and illuminating discussion *of le tragique féminin* (the female tragic), see ibid. *passim*. And, in a different context but with occasional references to Piaf, see

Barbara Lebrun, *Dalida: mythe et mémoire* (Marseille: Le Mot et le Reste, 2020).

21  Morizot, *Je les ai tous vus débuter*, 48.

22  Dumont, *Non,* 150.

23  Belleret, *Piaf,* 19.

24  *L'Olympia: le chantier du talent* (Paris: CPL, 1997), 7.

25  Ludovic Tournès, 'Reproduire l'œuvre: la nouvelle économie musicale', in *La Culture de masse en France de la Belle Époque à aujourd'hui,* ed. Jean-Pierre Rioux and Jean-François Sirinelli (Paris: Fayard, 2002), 225. The French term *tour de chant* is often mistranslated as a singing 'tour'. It actually means a stage act consisting of a singer (or singers) who delivers only songs rather than including other forms of entertainment. See Geneviève Beauvarlet and Lucien Rioux, 'Le Tour de chant', in *Music-hall et café-concert*, ed. André Sallée and Philippe Chauveau (Paris: Bordas, 1985), 36.

26  Beauvarlet and Rioux, 'Le Tour de chant', 36.

27  Verlant (ed.), *Olympia,* 24.

28  *L'Olympia*, 15.

29  Quoted in François Lévy, *Passion Édith Piaf: La Môme de Paris* (Paris: Textuel, 2003), 171.

30  Cited in Marchois, *La Vraie Piaf*, 149.

31  François Jouffa and Jacques Barsamian, *Johnny 60 ans* (Paris: L'Archipel, 2002), 47–65. Coquatrix later denied turning Johnny down and claimed to have no recollection of being asked: ibid., 49–51.

32  Ibid., 47.

33  Quoted in Verlant (ed.), *Olympia,* 59.

**34** In French there's a questionable tendency to lump Britain and the United States together under the historically vacuous label 'Anglo-Saxon'. It's a term I prefer to avoid; hence the inverted commas here.

**35** This dedication is often referred to, though it's difficult to find hard evidence of how or even whether she actually did so.

**36** In some accounts, a Legion representative was present at the funeral, but this is hard to verify.

**37** Légion Étrangère, 'La Musique de la Légion Étrangère rend hommage à Édith Piaf'. Available online: https://www.legion-etrangere.com/mdl/page.php?id=319 (accessed 31 January 2022).

**38** Looseley, *Édith Piaf*, 77–8.

**39** Alain Spiraux, 'Édith Piaf, comme la France' (*Combat*, 10 March 1959).

# Chapter 3

**1** 'Les industries musicales et électriques Pathé-Marconi' but usually abbreviated to just 'Pathé-Marconi'. That name was finally replaced with 'EMI France' in 1990.

**2** Joël Huthwohl, (ed.), *Piaf* (Paris: Bibliothèque Nationale de France), 2015, 155.

**3** In the burgeoning French record industry, the artistic director initially had an A&R function within a company but came to combine this, as the industry expanded, with a supervisory and sometimes creative role in the studio, closer to that of the record producer. Readers of French can learn more about this role in Ludovic Tournès, *Musique! Du phonographe au MP3*, rev. edn (Paris: Autrement, 2011), 48–50.

**4**   Tournès, 'Reproduire l'œuvre', 233.

**5**   The four songs were 'L'Étranger', 'Les Mômes de la cloche', 'La Java de Cézique' and 'Mon apéro'.

**6**   Tournès, *Musique!*, 74–5.

**7**   Her very first microgroove output actually dated from 1949 but it consisted only of compilations of her 78s for release in the United States.

**8**   Quoted in Marchois, *La Vraie Piaf*, 255.

**9**   Michel Rivgauche describes some of her recording habits in ibid., 426, but a number of other sources do too.

**10**   Céline Chabot-Canet, 'La Voix enregistrée dans la chanson française contemporaine: présence charnelle d'un corps virtuel', in *Chanson et performance: mise en scène du corps dans la chanson française et francophone*, ed. Barbara Lebrun (Paris: L'Harmattan, 2012), 21–3. Chabot-Canet, 23, makes use of Barthes's similar argument that the voice is present in the body and the body in the voice.

**11**   Stéphane Hirschi, *Chanson: l'art de fixer l'air du temps. De Béranger à Mano Solo* (Paris: Les Belles Lettres; Presses Universitaires de Valenciennes, 2008), 162–3.

**12**   I am indebted to my colleague at Leeds University, a specialist in French linguistics, Dr Nigel Armstrong, for clarifying this distinction.

**13**   Hirschi, *Chanson*, 130–5 (quotation, 131) and 159–64.

**14**   Ibid., 131–2.

**15**   Antoine Hennion, 'Music Lovers: Taste as Performance', *Theory, Culture and Society* 18 (October 2001): 5.

**16**   Charles Dumont, correspondence with the author, 22 June 2021.

**17** The page numbers I provide for each song refer the reader to the following book of lyrics: Pierre Saka (ed.), *Édith Piaf: L'Hymne à l'amour* (Paris: Le Livre de Poche, 1994).

**18** Until around 1968, it was common for French artists to release 45rpm extended plays of three or four tracks, rather than singles.

**19** See Saka (ed.), *Édith Piaf*, 307.

**20** Roland Barthes, *A Lover's Discourse: Fragments* (1978, London: Vintage, 2018), 6.

**21** Margaret Crosland, *A Cry from the Heart: The Life of Edith Piaf*, rev. edn (London: Arcadia, 2002), 166.

**22** See Saka (ed.), *Édith Piaf*, 121.

**23** Dumont, *Non*, 92.

**24** Carolyn Burke, *No Regrets: The Life of Édith Piaf*, paperback edn (London: Bloomsbury, 2012), 199.

**25** Albert Bensoussan, *Édith Piaf* (Paris: Gallimard, 2013), 181.

**26** I'm indebted to Professor Sue Miller for her help with describing the music here.

**27** For Piaf's performance of the song, I use both the audio version recorded on 29 December 1960 and an unattributed snippet of video on YouTube: https://youtu.be/sTZNhkwLWJE (accessed 20 February 2022).

# Chapter 4

**1** This song doesn't appear in Saka's book of lyrics.

**2** The soundtrack of Becker's black and white film even features a similarly mournful harmonica. I'm grateful to the anonymous reviewer of my manuscript who pointed this out.

**3** After struggling to think of a way of staging the song, Piaf emphasized this aspect by wearing a raincoat and walking across the width of the stage.

**4** The *Billboard* list for 5 June 1961, compiled by Eddie Adamis (See Chapter 2 n.2 above), also placed Piaf's song 'Exodus' at number 5. It is partly reproduced in Muz Hit! 'The French charts'.

**5** Quoted in Pierre Duclos and Georges Martin, *Piaf: biographie* (Paris: Seuil, 1993), 415.

**6** Dumont, *Non*, 98.

**7** Ibid., 119.

**8** Institut National de l'Audiovisuel. 'Édith Piaf, "Non, je ne regrette rien"'. Available online: https://www.ina.fr/ina-eclaire-actu/video/i00012768/edith-piaf-non-je-ne-regrette-rien (accessed 2 February 2022). This isn't her performance of 29 December 1960 but an earlier on-stage version shown on *Cinq colonnes à la une* on 2 December.

**9** 'Édith Piaf non je ne regrette rien, Olympia 18.01.1961' (that date is disputed). Available online: https://www.youtube.com/watch?v=iYvJa2jghLY (accessed 11 February 2022).

**10** Crosland, *A Cry*, 172.

**11** Noli, *Piaf secrète*, 78.

**12** Quoted in Marchois, *La Vraie Piaf*, 150.

# Chapter 5

**1** Quoted in 'Le Mythe Piaf'. *Le Point*, 1 February 2007. Available online: https://www.lepoint.fr/musique/le-mythe-piaf-01-02-2007-111252_38.php#xtmc=le-mythe-piaf&xtnp=1&xtcr=1 (accessed 2 February 2022).

**2** Allan Moore, 'Authenticity as Authentication', *Popular Music*
  21, no. 2 (2002): 214 and 220.

**3** Deniot, *Édith Piaf*, 133.

**4** Quoted in Manceaux, 'Piaf ressuscitée'.

**5** Ibid.

**6** Sarraute, 'Édith Piaf à l'Olympia'.

**7** Barthes's notes are reproduced in Huthwohl (ed.), *Piaf*, 78–9.

**8** Moore, 'Authenticity', 215.

**9** Benedict Anderson, *Imagined Communities: Reflections on
  the Origin and Spread of Nationalism*, rev. edn (London: Verso,
  2006).

**10** Burke, *No Regrets,* 202.

**11** Spiraux, 'Édith Piaf'.

**12** 'Le Mythe Piaf'.

**13** Catherine Rudent, 'Chanson Française: A Genre without
  Musical Identity', in *Made in France: Studies in Popular Music*,
  ed. Gérôme Guibert and Catherine Rudent (New York and
  Oxford: Routledge, 2018), 137–8 and 144–5.

**14** David Looseley, *Popular Music in Contemporary France:
  Authenticity, Politics, Debate* (Oxford and New York: Berg,
  2003), 63–86.

**15** Hirschi, *Chanson*, 146–7.

**16** Ibid., 191.

**17** *Cinq colonnes à la une*.

**18** Quoted in Sallée and Chauveau (eds) *Music-hall et café-
  concert* (Paris: Bordas, 1985), 69.

**19** Quoted in Lebrun, *Dalida*, 107.

**20** 'Le Mythe Piaf'. The French phrase used here, 'cette histoire
  française', is ambiguous. It could mean that Piaf's personal

'French story' has turned her into a realm of memory or that it is French history that has done so.

**21** Pierre Nora (ed.), *Realms of Memory: Rethinking the French Past*, rev. and abridged trans. Arthur Goldhammer (Columbia: Columbia University Press, 1996), xxiv.

**22** Ibid., 6.

**23** Édith Piaf, *The Wheel of Fortune: The Autobiography of Édith Piaf*, trans. Peter Trewartha and Andrée Masoin de Virion (London: Peter Owen, 2004).

**24** Lebrun, *Dalida*, 133.

**25** Burke, *No Regrets,* 200.

**26** Quoted in ibid., 201.

**27** Richard Dyer, *Stars*, New supplemented edn (Houndmills: Palgrave Macmillan, 1998).

**28** Edgar Morin, *The Stars*, trans. Richard Howard (Minneapolis and London: University of Minnesota Press, 2005).

**29** Tournès, *Musique!*, 94–5.

**30** Her friend Germain Ricord, quoted in Marchois, *La Vraie Piaf*, 413.

# Conclusions

**1** I'm grateful to Ewan Burnet for overhearing and passing on this anecdote.

**2** Huthwohl (ed.), *Piaf*, 146. Literally: a star thanks to records.

**3** Increasingly, the English word 'live' is used instead of *en direct*, as an adjective or noun designating a live recording or broadcast. A live album like *Récital 1961* might today be described as *un live*.

**4**   François Armanet and Bayon, *Haut les filles: le rock au féminin* (Paris: Flammarion, 2020). I have consulted only the book since it reprints the interviews in full. There's a doubly patronizing pun in the title, which roughly means 'Stand up girls' but also 'Oh girls!' (see note 5 below).

**5**   'Oh les filles! A film by François Armanet' [press release]. Available online: https://medias.unifrance.org/medias/15/36/205839/presse/haut-les-filles-dossier-de-presse-anglais.pdf (accessed 2 February 2022). This is the not entirely accurate English version of the press release but my quotation is my own translation from the French version.

**6**   Institut National de l'Audiovisuel, 'Merci Édith Piaf: 40 ans de la journée internationale des droits des femmes, 11.03.2017'. Available online: https://www.ina.fr/ina-eclaire-actu/video/vdx17000810/merci-edith-piaf (accessed 2 February 2022).

**7**   O'Brien, *She Bop*, 48.

**8**   Culture Trip, 'Ten Women Who Changed French History'. Available online: https://theculturetrip.com/europe/france/paris/articles/10-women-who-changed-french-history (accessed 2 February 2022).

# Bibliography

Adamis, Eddie. 'French News Notes: French Digging US Jazz Wax'. *Billboard Music Week*, 14.

Anderson, Benedict. *Imagined Communities: Reflections on the Origin and Spread of Nationalism*. Rev. edn. London: Verso, 2006.

Armanet, François and Bayon. *Haut les filles: le rock au féminin*. Paris: Flammarion, 2020.

Barthes, Roland. *A Lover's Discourse: Fragments*. Trans. Richard Howard. 1978. Translation reissued. London: Vintage, 2018.

Beauvarlet, Geneviève and Lucien Rioux. 'Le Tour de chant'. In *Music-hall et café-concert*, edited by André Sallée and Philippe Chauveau, pp. 36–8. Paris: Bordas, 1985.

Belleret, Robert. *Piaf: un mythe français*. Paris: Fayard, 2013.

Bensoussan, Albert. *Édith Piaf*. Paris: Gallimard, 2013.

Bonini, Emmanuel. *Piaf: la vérité*. Paris: Pygmalion, 2008.

Bret, David. *Édith Piaf The Untold Story: Find Me a New Way to Die*. London: Oberon Books, 2015.

Burke, Carolyn. *No Regrets: The Life of Édith Piaf*. Paperback edition. London: Bloomsbury, 2012.

Chabot-Canet, Céline. 'La Voix enregistrée dans la chanson française contemporaine: présence charnelle d'un corps virtuel'. In *Chanson et performance: mise en scène du corps dans la chanson française et francophone*, edited by Barbara Lebrun, pp. 21–33. Paris: L'Harmattan, 2012.

*Cinq colonnes à la une* [TV programme]. Interview with Piaf. RTF. 2 December 1960. Available at www.ina.fr/video/I00000109/edith-piaf-avant-sanouvelle-tournee-video.html (accessed 2 February 2022).

Crosland, Margaret. *A Cry from the Heart: The Life of Edith Piaf*. Rev. edn. London: Arcadia, 2002.

Culture Trip, 'Ten Women Who Changed French History'. Available online: https://theculturetrip.com/europe/france/paris/articles/10-women-who-changed-french-history (accessed 2 February 2022).

Deniot, Joëlle-Andrée, *Édith Piaf la voix, le geste, l'icône: esquisse anthropologique*. Paris: Lelivredart, 2012.

*Discorama* [TV programme]. Interview with Piaf by Paul Giannoli. 20 January 1961. Not broadcast. Available at https://www.ina.fr/ina-eclaire-actu/video/cpf03007301/edith-piaf (accessed 28 January 2022).

Duclos, Pierre and Georges Martin. *Piaf: Biographie*. Paris: Seuil, 1993.

Dumont, Charles. *Non, je ne regrette toujours rien*. Paris: Calmann-Lévy, 2012.

Dumont, Charles. Correspondence with the author, 22 June 2021.

Dyer, Richard. *Stars*. New supplemented ed. Houndmills: Palgrave Macmillan, 1998.

'Édith Piaf non je ne regrette rien, Olympia 18.01.1961'. Available online: https://www.youtube.com/watch?v=iYvJa2jghLY (accessed 11 February 2022).

Ferment, Fabrice. Correspondence with the author, 25 November–13 December 2021.

Gurgand, Jean-Noël. 'Édith Piaf: la boucle est bouclée'. *France Observateur*, 5 January 1961.

Hennion, Antoine. 'Music Lovers: Taste as Performance'. *Theory, Culture and Society* 18 (October 2001): 1–22.

Hirschi, Stéphane. *Chanson: l'art de fixer l'air du temps. De Béranger à Mano Solo*. Paris: Les Belles Lettres; Presses Universitaires de Valenciennes, 2008.

Huthwohl, Joël (ed.). *Piaf*. Paris: Bibliothèque Nationale de France, 2015.

Institut National de l'Audiovisuel. 'Édith Piaf, "Non, je ne regrette rien"'. Available online: https://www.ina.fr/ina-eclaire-actu/video/i00012768/edith-piaf-non-je-ne-regrette-rien (accessed 2 February 2022).

Institut National de l'Audiovisuel. 'Haut les filles: Et si le rock n'était pas né avec Elvis Presley, mais avec Édith Piaf? Available online: https://www.ina.fr/actualites-ina/haut-les-filles (accessed 2 February 2022).

Institut National de l'Audiovisuel. 'Merci Edith Piaf: 40 ans de la journée internationale des droits des femmes, 11.03.2017'. Available online: https://www.ina.fr/ina-eclaire-actu/video/vdx17000810/merci-edith-piaf (accessed 2 February 2022).

Jouffa, François and Jacques Barsamian, *Johnny 60 Ans*, Paris: L'Archipel, 2002.

Lebrun, Barbara. *Dalida: mythe et mémoire*. Marseille: Le Mot et le Reste, 2020.

Légion Étrangère, 'La Musique de la Légion Étrangère rend hommage à Édith Piaf'. Available online: https://www.legion-etrangere.com/mdl/page.php?id=319 (accessed 31 January 2022).

Leuzinger, Pierre. 'Résurrection de Piaf'. *Tribune de Genève*, 7 January 1961.

Lévy, François, *Passion Édith Piaf: La Môme de Paris*. Paris: Textuel, 2003.

Looseley, David. *Popular Music in Contemporary France: Authenticity, Politics, Debate*. Oxford and New York: Berg, 2003.

Looseley, David. *Édith Piaf: A Cultural History*. Liverpool: Liverpool University Press, 2015.

Manceaux, Michèle. 'Piaf ressuscitée'. *L'Express*, 4 January 1961.

Marchois, Bernard. *Piaf: emportée par la foule*. Paris: Éditions du Collectionneur; Vade Retro,1993.

Marchois, Bernard. *La Vraie Piaf: témoignages et portraits inédits*. Paris: Éditions Didier Carpentier, 2013.

Moore, Allan. 'Authenticity as Authentication'. *Popular Music* 21, no. 2 (2002): 209–23.

Morin, Edgar. *The Stars*. Trans. Richard Howard. Minneapolis and London: University of Minnesota Press, 2005.

Morizot, Doudou (with Emmanuel Bonini). *Je les ai tous vus débuter*. Paris: L'Archipel, 2021.

Morizot, Doudou. Correspondence with the author, undated (February 2022).

Muz Hit! 'The French Charts Are Celebrating Their 35th Anniversary. Or Is It Their 58th?'. Available online: https://muzhit.com/?p=384 (accessed 1 February 2022).

'Le Mythe Piaf'. *Le Point*, 1 February 2007. Available online: https://www.lepoint.fr/musique/le-mythe-piaf-01-02-2007-111252_38.php#xtmc=le-mythe-piaf&xtnp=1&xtcr=1 (accessed 2 February 2022).

Noli, Jean. *Piaf secrète*. Paris: L'Archipel, 1973.

Nora, Pierre (ed.). *Realms of Memory: Rethinking the French Past*. Revised and abridged trans. Arthur Goldhammer. Columbia: Columbia University Press, 1996.

O'Brien, Lucy. *She Bop: The Definitive History of Women in Popular Music*. Rev. edn (25th anniversary edition). London: Jawbone, 2020.

'Oh les filles! A film by François Armanet' [press release]. Available online: https://medias.unifrance.org/medias/15/36/205839/ presse/haut-les-filles-dossier-de-presse-anglais.pdf (accessed 2 February 2022).

*L'Olympia: le chantier du talent*. Paris: CPL, 1997.

Piaf, Édith. *My Life*. Trans. M. Crosland. London: Penguin, 1992.

Piaf, Édith. *The Wheel of Fortune: The Autobiography of Édith Piaf*. Trans. Peter Trewartha and Andrée Masoin de Virion. London: Peter Owen, 2004.

Robine, Marc. *Il était une fois la chanson française*. Paris: Fayard/ Livre de Poche, 2004.

Rudent, Catherine. 'Chanson Française: A Genre without Musical Identity'. In *Made in France: Studies in Popular Music*, edited by Gérome Guibert and Catherine Rudent, pp. 137–49. New York and Oxford: Routledge, 2018.

Sallée, Albert and Philippe Chauveau (eds). *Music-hall et café-concert*. Paris: Bordas, 1985.

Sarraute, Claude. 'Édith Piaf à l'Olympia'. *Le Monde*, 31 December 1960.

Spiraux, Alain. 'Édith Piaf, comme la France'. *Combat*, 10 March 1959.

Tournès, Ludovic. 'Reproduire l'œuvre: la nouvelle économie musicale'. In *La Culture de masse en France de la Belle Époque à aujourd'hui*, edited by Jean-Pierre Rioux and Jean-François Sirinelli, pp. 220–58. Paris: Fayard, 2002.

Tournès, Ludovic. *Musique! Du phonographe au MP3*. Rev. edn. Paris: Autrement, 2011.

Vassal, Hugues. *Dans les pas de … Édith Piaf*. Paris: Les Trois
    Orangers, 2002.

Vassal, Hugues. *Dans l'intimité des stars de la chanson*. Paris:
    L'Archipel, 2019.

Vassal, Hugues, 'Dans l'intimité des stars, le spectacle'. Available
    online: https://www.hugues-vassal.com/show-biz (accessed
    4 February 2022).

Verlant, Gilles (ed.). *Olympia Bruno Coquatrix: 50 ans de music-hall*.
    Paris: Éditions Hors Collection, 2003.

# Index

It clearly isn't practical to list all references to Piaf, the recital, the album or the Olympia, as some appear on virtually every page. There is an entry for the Olympia, which directs readers only to those pages dealing with its history and significance. Piaf's songs are listed individually by title, with any definite or indefinite articles placed at the end of the reference (for example, 'Accordéoniste L''). The individual sections discussing the nine tracks on the album in Chapters 3 and 4 are indicated in italics. Songs by others are listed by performer; films and plays by director or playwright. I have only indexed lyricists and composers of Piaf songs when they appear in the body of the text, rather than when titles are merely attributed to them. I have included the names of figures of cultural significance even when they appear only fleetingly, as these might help the reader track or contextualize Piaf's global standing, in the past and in the present.

Index